Genesis II

The Re-Creation of Black People

Glenda,
Love & Blessings,
Thank you,
Dr. Shelley
2019

Genesis II

The Re-Creation of Black People

Cardinal Monifa Imarogbe

Africa World Press, Inc.

P.O. Box 1892
Trenton, NJ 08607

P.O. Box 48
Asmara, ERITREA

Africa World Press, Inc.

P.O. Box 1892
Trenton, NJ 08607

P.O. Box 48
Asmara, ERITREA

Book design: Krystal Jackson
Cover design: Debbie Hird
Cover illustration by Carl Owens. Portrait of Black Madonna displayed at Shrine Nine in Atlanta

Library of Congress Cataloging-in-Publication data

McIntosh, Shelly
GenesisII: the re-creation of black people/ Monifa Imarogbe
p. cm.
Includes bibliographical references and index
ISBN: 0-86543-873-0 - - ISBN: 0-86543-874-9 (pbk.)
I. Black theology. 2. Liberation theology. 3. Bible- -Black interpretations
4. Pan African Orthodox Christian Church--Doctrines. I. Title: Genesis 2.II. Title: Genesis two III. Title

BT82.7 .M39 2000
230'089'96 - - dc21 00-056580

Dedicated to my husband, Awznee.

To Cardinal Olu (I know you are resting with the ancestors), and to my children, Lateefah and Italo

Contents

PREFACE

This book contains a collection of Black Theology bible lessons presented to the congregation and visitors of the Shrines of the Black Madonna of the Pan African Orthodox Christian Church. Black or liberation theology is emphasized because of the simple fact that the basic problem facing the Black church is a theological one. The Black church is in conflict because it has adopted a gospel of salvation rather than a gospel of liberation. The two are not the same and it is impossible to build a Black Nation without rejecting the gospel of salvation which is an individualistic otherworldly conception of salvation—preaching that salvation is the free gift of God, made available to those who believe by the sacrifice of Jesus on Calvary, and that we are saved by faith and not by works. Because of this theology, the Black church has programmed people to believe in individual salvation resulting in our own gross neglect of the needs of Black people on a whole. Since the gospel of salvation espouses faith rather than works, thousands of Black people do not commit themselves to the necessary work it takes to build a nation for ourselves. Our potential collective power is left at ground zero due to each of us individually trying to get to heaven while our collective oppressive condition on earth is growing increasingly worse.

On the other hand, with the gospel of liberation everything is defined in terms of the Black Liberation Struggle. We seek to end our earthly oppression so anything that supports this is deemed relevant and good. The basis of the gospel of liberation can be found in the life and teachings of Jesus, the Black Messiah; not in his death, but in his life and in his willingness to die for the Black Nation Israel. God reconciled men unto Himself in the life and teachings of Jesus, which gave men a new conception of human dignity and inspired them to fight to be men instead of slaves. God was in Jesus and He can be in anyone who is willing to dedicate his/her life to the Liberation Struggle.

These lessons are based on the historical struggles of the Black Nation Israel, its covenant relationship with God, the teachings of the Law and the prophets, and the revolutionary mission of Jesus, the Black Messiah. The ideas were discussed in meetings chaired by Reverend Albert B. Cleage, Jr. and attended by a group of ministers. Correct interpretation of the bible, in that it is a liberation document, was emphasized and clarified. Imperative in all discussions was the theme of Genesis II, the transformation of Black people which is possible through the acceptance of a liberation theology. If Black people can believe that God works with us as a people, and that it is God's will for us to build power for ourselves, then the chasm between God and man can be bridged. Each lesson has a specific scriptural passage, a Bible lesson that interprets the scripture, and three specific points. The development of which is done by biblical history, history of Black people, conditions in the present world, and constructive criticisms of Black behaviors and attitudes. My life, as well as countless others, have been transformed through rejection of individualism, the practice of communalism, and the experience of God as taught in the gospel of liberation by the Pan African Orthodox Christian Church. Our beliefs as well as our works are now relevant to the building of a better world for Black people.

I was moved by the spirit to make a contribution to transmitting the gospel of liberation as taught to me by Jaramogi Abebe Agyeman (Reverend Albert B. Cleage, Jr.). I feel deeply that he is the messenger of truth. It is my hope that this book continues the comprehensive knowledge so portrayed by Jaramogi, and inspires Black churches to become instrumental in changing the conditions of Black people. I have supplied the following pertinent information in hopes to create a context that will bring more understanding to the lessons. It includes a brief introduction of Jaramogi, and a series of questions and answers pertaining to the concept of Genesis II.

Jaramogi Abebe Agyeman, (Reverend Albert B. Cleage, Jr.) is the Father of Black Theology, and the Founder of the Shrines of the Black Madonna of the Pan African Orthodox Christian Church established in 1953. In 1971, he wrote the controversial book entitled *The Black Messiah*, a series of sermons that expressed the historical blackness of Jesus and his revolutionary mission. His second book, *Black Christian Nationalism, New Directions for the Black Church*, written in 1972, explained in depth the struggles of the Black Nation Israel, the theology of the bible and how it relates to Black Christian Nationalism, and how the Black church could become instrumental to the survival of Black people. In addition, that book pointed out that Christianity is a Black man's religion, relevant to our struggle for freedom and dignity. In 1985, Jaramogi gave the following riveting analysis and prophecy of mankind in his discourse entitled "Genesis II: The Recreation of the Black Man."

Can human society survive? Human society cannot survive without a conscious restructuring of its basic foundations. Total commitment to communalism as a way of life, and acceptance of the Unified Field concept of God's power in the world are essential corner stones of the New Order. We recognize individualism as a global cancer, which has infected and contaminated the whole of human life.

What is the economic future of the West? The society of which we are part is on a collision course with disaster. The computer has made possible technological changes, which are transforming an industrial society into an information society requiring basic changes in the way people live. Cybernetics and robotics are making most unskilled and uneducated workers obsolete. Unemployment is no longer a temporary inconvenience and there are few resources for social service assistance by governmental agencies which are finding it impossible to adjust to urgent human demands of this chaotic period of transition into a post industrial era.

Technological changes have given rise not only to economic dislocation consisting of mass unemployment and outmoded factories no longer able to compete in world markets, but have led to the rise of new non-national conglomerates able to seek out the cheapest labor supply any place in the world. Big labor unions can no longer protect a worker's job from the computer chip or from cheap third world labor. Labor unions are doomed as are the large cities which exist to house and service laborers who assemble to work in the huge industrial plants which are now being automated and moved away from old decaying crime infested urban centers which have already been taken over by poor, uneducated and unskilled Black workers.

What is the future of the working class? The ordinary mass man can no longer enjoy a secure "second class" existence. He is doomed to extinction. His survival within the system has become impossible. The stress of life on the borderline of disaster, trying to hold on to the futile dream of happiness and success will destroy him! Only frustration and escapism will remain.

How has slavery and oppression affected Black people? As Black people, we live in a "slave culture," a sub-culture of the powerless who have been declared inferior and excluded from full participation in the dominate culture of the oppressor. Without the power to actually reproduce the culture from which he has been excluded, the Black man is content to live in a world of make believe where life becomes a "celebration of inferiority."

How has the acceptance of the myth of Black inferiority affected Black people? Our acceptance of inferiority cannot be consciously admitted so we repress it, leaving it to function as unconscious motivation. We reject our Blackness and seek to build a fantasy identity with which to conceal it. This is the Black man's identity problem.

A Black man living in a white world, which has declared him inferior, cannot escape the stigma of his blackness. There is no escape as an individual. Only a group can create a counter culture in which Black is acceptable. Because you are Black, you live in a ghetto with all of its restrictions; poverty, unemployment, crime, exploitation, poor schools, social disorganization, and powerless dependency; you resent being Black with all of its restrictions so you try to break your identification by denying your identity. You try to pretend that you are not black.

What must Black people do to survive? The Black man must extricate himself from destructive elements of Black life if he is to survive. First, he must end his dependence upon the white man's corrupt world order. It is still possible for the Black man to break away and be saved. Breaking away involves the total rejection of individualism and the total acceptance of communalism. This means voluntary separation from the white individualistic world. Second, he must end the vicious effects of second-class citizenship with its self-perpetuating cycle of ignorance, poverty, and powerlessness. He must build a Black counter culture able to provide self-created opportunities, which will enable the Black man to build Black institutions to serve the needs of Black people. This will only be possible if the Black man can reject individualism and utilize fully the power of communalism. Third, the destructive element of Black life provided by the slave culture must be completely destroyed. The Black man must accept a totally new life-style, time-ritual and value system dictated by the needs of communal living.

How should we understand God, man and creation? In the beginning, nothing existed but the power and creative intelligence of God. Out of a mystical explosion of divine energy, the cosmos and everything in it was created. This act of creation provided an orderly unification of the four fundamental forces of nature in a Unified Field controlling the functions and interaction of all things. It took some fifteen billion years from the moment of divine creation for mankind to evolve into a recognizable human form on the continent of Africa. Whether or not a similar evolutionary process produced human beings on other planets or in other galaxies, we have no way of knowing. From the moment of creation, human beings with God-given freedom of the will, have carried the individualistic seed of ultimate self-destruction, and human society has been on a downward spiral toward total individualism and the concentration of wealth, education and power in the hands of fewer and fewer people. So, a totally individualistic society revolves around the whims and appetites of the few who use their control of wealth and the means of production to control the political, industrial and military complexes upon which life depends.

What is the Pan African Orthodox Christian Church? The P.A.O.C.C. is a realistic Black Liberation Movement built upon the authentic spiritual relations and experiences of the sons and daughters of our motherland Africa, the historical revelations of the Black Nation Israel, and the life and teachings of the Black Messiah, Jesus. Those who join must reject identification with their White oppressor and break all ties with the slave culture. This break must be "cold turkey," clean and complete.

What is the Transforming Community? It is the Sacred Circle within which the presence of God can be invoked and is the basis upon which the P.A.O.C.C. undertakes to build a new world for Black people, a "Nation within a Nation."

We acknowledge our wretched condition, the evil nature of the enemy system, which shapes our lives, and the inner sickness, which tortures us with a conditioned self, which we can no longer control.

What are the goals of the P.A.O.C.C.? Created by God and conditioned by an evil society, we have lost the integration of Spirit, Mind and Body. We now seek to find wholeness and the maximum activation of our God-given human powers by rejecting an evil world and becoming part of a Transforming Community in which we can be changed. The radical change, which we seek, constitutes, in fact, the re-creation of man, and the creation of a new world order.

How is the Transforming Community related to Genesis II? The Transforming Community is the matrix in which life can be completely reorganized through the utilization of God-power, which becomes available to us when we rise above the limitations of the rational mind. The infinite unimaginable Godpower of the Unified Field, in which the four fundamental forces of nature are unified, controls all of the inter-related aspects of the cosmos and offers human society, within the boundaries of the Sacred Circle, all possibilities for the re-creation of man, the creation of an ideal new world order.

There must be no ambiguity about **Genesis II**. It is a revolutionary program designed to build an ideal Nation for Black people here on earth, a counter culture that rejects the individualism and inequities of the Western World and builds upon the historic roots of the Pan-African God-experience.

The **Genesis II** program has been greatly developed over the past fifteen years in the area of human transformation through socialization, moving people from individualism to communalism, and by the actual experience of God. Involving people in group sessions, and structuring the equitable distribution of tasks, affection, and spiritual energy as the foundation of group life have assisted this change. The Science of KUA is the process of self-actualization of becoming what you already are, and it entails all the practices of group life including communal living, devotionals, sacramental worship, KUA workshops (invocation, yoga, Tai Chi, meditation), and rituals. KUA has been implemented into the total life of the church impacting the very young and the elderly. KUA opens groups to Godpower. It is the foundation of Genesis II, transforming Black people so they can transform their earthly conditions.

In this first volume, the theme is the quest for God, which is the initial step in Genesis II. The experience of God transforms thus recreating the Black man. Also, emphasis is placed on the belief that one must be open to God and community for both his/her salvation and survival. The lessons, which move from the individual quest to the vision and quest of a people, inexplicably connect spiritualism with nation building. Although addressed to African-American congregations, there are basic truths that apply to all mankind.

Genesis II

ACKNOWLEDGMENTS

My sincere gratitude goes to Fundi Fabu. Her perseverance, ideas, organization of bible lessons, editing, and time have allowed for the completion of this book. I cherish her sacrifices greatly. Fundi Akita and Lieutenant Imara provided the graphic art ideas and Imara spent a great deal of time researching and organizing the illustrations. Your support is priceless. Thanks to Cardinal Nandi, an original founder of the Pan African Orthodox Christian Church, who inspires and motivates us to continue the struggle. Dr. Pamela Norwood, who supported this endeavor and sacrificially read over the original manuscript advising me to clarify how the reader was to interact with the text. You are an inspiration. Appreciation to the Assembly of Cardinals: Cardinals Kimathi, Mbiyu, Omodele, and Abi. Those discussions, though sometimes intense, were needed. Great love to my mother and father, Ruth and Rufus Miller, who attempted to give their children a strong foundation in caring for others and in obeying God. Thank you for giving me life and being such caring parents.

Thanks to the many church members and children of the Shrine of the Black Madonna who have taught me about myself and made my life complete. A special appreciation for my husband, Awznee who read over my lessons and offered constructive criticism, and whose patience allowed me to work quietly even though he wanted to talk at times. Great appreciation to Jaramogi, who led us in many discussions concerning the truths of the bible and the purposes and goals of the Church. These words are inadequate in expressing my deepest gratitude and appreciation, for he has saved, transformed, and given hope to thousands in sharing his vision of a strong Black Nation. I love you Jaramogi and I miss you greatly. All honor given to God, my Creator and Guide.

GLOSSARY

The following terms are defined for your understanding. I have included them at the beginning rather than the end.

ABI. Acceptance of the myth of black inferiority.

Alkebu-lan Academy. The name of the youth program derived from the ancient name of Africa,which is Alkebu-lan. It is pronounced, *Al-ke-boo-land.*

BCN. Black Christian Nationalism, the revealed truth upon which the Pan-African Orthodox Christian Church is founded and the gospel of redemption for a world in bondage to sin. Members of the Pan African Orthodox Christian church are *Black Christian Nationalists.*

BCN Code. A simplified basic statement of the day-to-day behavioral requirements for BCN membership as outlined in the BCN Creed, Program, Position and Teachings and explained in The Black Messiah and Black Christian Nationalism.

Beulah Land. 2,800 acres of land acquired by the sacrifices of Church members; housing, agriculture, and schools are major developments to assist Black people in becoming self-sufficient; the Promised Land.

Black Nation Israel. A clan of African people whose history is told in the Bible.

Communalism. A way of life in which the goals and welfare of a group of people are more important than individual desires. It is characterized by the equitable distribution of tasks, affection, and spiritual energy. This value is based upon biblical truth and the practices of the first Christian Church of Jesus' Disciples.

Cultural Center. An institution/store of the church, which glorifies the African culture of Black people. It contains books, African jewelry, art, clothing, cards and a friendly and "at home" atmosphere. The cultural centers are located in Detroit, Michigan; Atlanta, Georgia; and Houston, Texas.

DBI An acronym for the myth of the declaration of Black inferiority. Theory developed by White society that Black people are innately inferior.

Devotional. A systematic, seven step process that opens individuals to the experience of God through a sustained group experience. It lasts about three hours and it includes invocation, discourse on the nature of God, Covenant relationship and the fact that we are sinners, confession and absolution, awareness, massage, and Yoga and meditation.

Divine Obligations. Acts of commitment such as work, tithes, and evangelism.

Individualism. Self-centered, egocentric, and selfish human behavior. It is the lower nature of man and judged as sin for it negates innate human value.

Institution. A structure developed by a group to transmit power for that particular group (schools, hospitals, industries, etc.)

Jaramogi Abebe Agyeman. The Holy Patriarch and founder of the Pan African Orthodox Christian Church (PAOCC), Reverend Albert B. Cleage, Jr. It is pronounced, *Jer-ah-moe-ji, Ah-bay-bay- Ah-ji-men.*

Kazi. Communal work engaged in by all members for the maintenance and upkeep of property and institutions. It is pronounced, *Ka-zee*.

Kodi. Voluntary taxation, financial commitment to the church. It is pronounced, *Ko-dee*.

KUA. The Science of Becoming What You Already Are. The Christian Science of Self-Actualization. It is pronounced, *Ku-ah*.

Kugasana. We experience the power of God.

Kujitoa. We are in total submission to the will of God.

Kusanya Watu. Bringing Black people together by means of inviting them into the Church community. Another term is Community Outreach. It is pronounced, *Ku-san-yah Wah-too*.

Kutafuta. We seek the experience of God.

Kutamungu. We can come upon God here where we are.

Kuumba Kitchen. A dining facility/institution of the Church in which members share communal meals. It is pronounced, *Koo-oom-bah*.

Liberation. Freedom from control and domination by another group.

Maccabees. Security group of the Church, named after original Maccabees of biblical times.

MTI. An acronym for Missionary Training Institutes; apartment complexes owned and operated by the Church and serving as a safe, communal environment in which members voluntarily live and engage in the activities of the church for training.

Mtoto House. A children's institution of the Church. Designed on the basis of group living. Children reside in dormitory arrangements for group and spiritual development.

Nation. A group of people united to obtain or perpetuate their power.

Pan Africanism. Concept of oneness of African people across the world organizing where they reside to build international power for African people.

Power. Control over the institutional structure that governs a group's life.

Slave. One who is part of a group whose total existence is controlled by another group.

Slave Culture. Lifestyle developed by an oppressed group that has psychologically accepted their conditions.

THE QUEST

We must find the ancient Disciplines used by Seekers in every generation...for the power of GOD to enter into us, to Enlighten us, and to Transform us."

—Jaramogi

SANKOFA: Go back and fetch it

"But when the king came in to see the guests, he noticed a man there who was not wearing a wedding robe, and he said to him, 'Friend, how did you get in here without a wedding robe?' And he was speechless. Then the king said to the attendants, 'Bind him hand and foot, and throw him into the outer darkness, where there will be weeping and gnashing of teeth.' For many are called, but few are chosen."

(Matthew 22: 11-14)

Bible Lesson: Jesus taught the parable of the wedding feast after his triumphal entry into Jerusalem. He taught in the temple because his disciples had taken it over as a political rebellion against Roman authority. Jesus begins, *"The Kingdom of Heaven may be compared to a king who gave a wedding banquet for his son."* The king prepared a great feast, and had issued invitations in advance. He sent his slaves out to call those who had been invited, but they did not come. After hearing this, the king sent his slaves out again with a message that everything was ready for the feast, but the people went home or continued to take care of their own business while others seized the king's slaves and killed them. The king was angry, so he sent out his troops to destroy the murderers and burn their city. The king said, *"The wedding is ready, but those invited were not wor-*

thy." Go into the streets and invite everyone you find. His slaves did this, and finally, the wedding hall was full. As the king came in to see the guests, his eyes fell upon one man who was not dressed appropriately. He asked the man, how did he get in without a wedding robe? The man had no explanation. The king told his attendants to throw him into the outer darkness. *Many are called, but few are chosen.*

Interpretation: The King is God, and the Son is Jesus, the Black Messiah. The Wedding Banquet is God's Kingdom, the Messianic Community on earth. It is the union of God with His chosen people. The guests were the people of the Black Nation Israel. God gave the invitation (call), but some paid no attention and continued on with their lives as usual. Some disdained the invitation so much that they killed the messengers. Inviting everyone they could find reflects the mercy of God and the desire that humankind return to Him. The man who did not attend in the wedding robe reflects the attitude of many who feel they do not have to meet any obligations to remain in the Kingdom of God. Throwing out the man in outer darkness symbolizes God's awareness of man, and man's responsibility to change. If man refuses to change, he will live in evil. *Many are called, but few are chosen.*

Jesus Sought the Experience of God Because of His Faith in the Covenant

The Quest: Jesus sought the experience of God when he left Nazareth and walked the dangerous Jericho Road to Jerusalem to be baptized in the Jordan River where he heard the voice of God declare him to be the Messiah, and a dove lighting upon his shoulder symbolized the fact that he had received the Holy Spirit. (2nd KUA Affirmation, Jaramogi).

Why would Jesus walk this dangerous road to Jerusalem? We must examine his life. From a small child, Jesus was taught that God is Power and Energy. *"Ascribe power to God, Whose majesty is over Israel; and Whose power is in the skies. Awesome is God in His sanctuary, the God of Israel; He gives power and strength to His people"* (Psalm 68: 34-35). From a small child, he was taught the Covenant, the Law, and the prophets. The prophet Jeremiah writes, *"In those days and in that time, says the Lord, the people of Israel shall come, they and the people of Judah together; they shall come weeping as they seek the Lord their God. They shall ask the way to Zion, with faces turned toward it, and they shall come and join themselves to the Lord by an everlasting covenant that will never be forgotten"* (Jeremiah 50:4-5). As a small child and undoubtedly as a young man, he witnessed the exploitation and persecution of his people by the Romans. He, too, heard the devout pray for God's intervention. *"Blessed be the Lord God of Israel, for He has looked favorably on His people and redeemed them. He has raised up a mighty savior for us."* (Luke 1: 68-69). Jesus' belief in the Covenant drove him to leave his home in Galilee in order to find God.

Where did Jesus go in hopes of experiencing God? He went to a group, the movement of John the Baptist that was a repentant, revolutionary, and righteous community. John called his people to repentance and to fulfill their obligations of the Covenant. John baptized Jesus. In Jesus' submergence in the water, his old life died and in his emergence from the water, he was born again into the Covenant relationship with God. It was here he experienced God as Power, and was anointed the Messiah, the Liberator of Israel. *"For many are called but few are chosen."*

Our Quest to Find God Grows Out of Our Acceptance of the Covenant

Acceptance of the Covenant is basic to our quest for the experience of God. This belief in the Covenant internally molds our values and attitudes, which inspire us to seek the Power, which created us. Without acceptance of the Covenant, we are like tumbleweeds carried away by every gust of wind; like a flower with no roots; like a house built on shaky ground. Acceptance of the Covenant builds our life's foundation. Like a tree planted by waters, we shall not be moved. It is the initial step towards total commitment.

When we joined the Church, God called us, just as the king invited guests to the wedding banquet. God, through His servant Jaramogi and the commitment of a few, prepared a place for us where love, safety, and peace abide .... The Kingdom of God on earth, just as the king prepared a great feast for the guests.

After joining, we were required to renounce an evil world and to abide by the LAW (BCN Code), behavior norms which fulfill our Covenant relationship with God, just like the guests who had to disrobe of their outer clothing, and put on a wedding robe fit for the occasion. To live in the Kingdom requires obedience to God's will just like the guests who were now required to adhere to the king's standards. To be obedient requires loyalty to God, which is only expressed through our acceptance of the Covenant. The Covenant then becomes our internal, driving motivation to seek God. It is at this point, we become enlightened to the revelations of God as structured in the activities of this Church. The group, the worship service, the devotionals, Kazi and divine obligations constitute the "Road" to experience God, and we grow keenly aware of this. Divine meanings are given to this way of life, which has been passed down by word of mouth through a thousand generations.

Like the man who attended the banquet without a wedding robe, we are adamant about living an old lifestyle with its worldly values. We are flagrant in our lack of participation, selfish with our skills and income, and blind to the reality that God has been keeping His end of the Covenant by providing us a heaven on earth built more by the sacrifices of others than by our own. The king looked for some change in his guests, just like God expects us to change. Be aware that your decisions either keep you in favor with God, or toss you in the outer darkness of an evil world.

The Practice of KUA Empowers Us to Build the Kingdom of God on Earth

As Black Christian Nationalists, we profess to be disciples of Jesus, the Black Messiah. In doing so, we are required to seek the experience of God. Jaramogi says, "For us the Experience of God is the basis of a revolutionary struggle for self-actualization and social change designed to transform our wretched Black condition here on earth. It is the basis for our commitment to the struggle.

It is not an end in itself." In light of this, our very survival depends on this church community experiencing the Power of God. "We experience God in the fellowship of the Church" (Jaramogi). It is only in the fellowship we learn to belong and to become a part of "the community"...to drop defenses...to love freely...to consider the needs of the Group more important than our own. KUA provides the way for us to do this. The first step in KUA is Socialization in which we move from individualism to communalism. We do this through total participation in the program of the Church, which opens us to others and to the Power of God. This participation is the PRACTICE OF KUA. It changes us as "*we pledge our total commitment to the task of rebuilding a Black Nation with power, here on earth*" (BCN Covenant) "*Like Jesus, we too, seek the experience of God. Kutafuta. Kutamungu. Kugasana. Kujitoa.*"

"DO LITTLE" CHRISTIANS

"If we are to seek, we must change,
Rejecting individualism,
Discarding false fronts, facing the repressions
Which conceal our guilt and deaden our pain."
—Jaramogi

KRAMO BONE AMMA YEAHU KRAMO PA:
Caution against deception and hypocrisy
We learn better out of truth

"Do not think that I have come to abolish the law or the prophets I have come not to abolish but to fulfill. Therefore, whoever breaks one of the least of these commandments, and teaches others to do the same, will be called least in the kingdom of heaven; but whoever does them and teaches them will be called great in the kingdom of heaven. For I tell you, unless your righteousness exceeds that of the scribes and Pharisees, you will never enter the kingdom of heaven."
(Matthew 5:17-20)

Bible Lesson: When Jesus began his revolutionary movement of uniting his people to fulfill their responsibility of maintaining their Covenant with God, and to free them from Roman oppression, he states what his mission is to minimize any confusion. Crowds follow him, and he speaks to them. *"Do not think that I have come to abolish the law or the prophets."* The law, given to Moses by God and passed down from generation to generation, is the behavior required to maintain the Covenant relationship with God. It includes the Ten Commandments and requirements of daily living. *"I am the Lord your God who brought you out of the land of Egypt, out of the house of slavery; you shall have no other gods before Me"* (Exodus 20). In addition, there were laws concerning the altar, property, restitution, social living and religious practices. This social religious structure, when adhered to, made Israel a righteous people, and evidenced their commitment to keep the Covenant. The prophets were the spiritual mouthpieces of God. Isaiah, Jeremiah, Ezekiel, Daniel, Hosea and others accepted the mission of teaching and prophesying to Israel. *"The word that came to Jeremiah from the Lord: Hear the words of this covenant, and speak to the people of Judah: 'Cursed be anyone who does not heed the words of this covenant, which I commanded your ancestors....Listen to My voice and do all that I command you. So shall you be My people, and I will be your God"* (Jeremiah 11:3-5). Jesus said, *"I have come to fulfill the Law and the prophets."*

Jesus teaches the crowds and his disciples that their righteousness must exceed that of the Pharisees to clear up further confusion. He tells his disciples to do whatever the Pharisees teach you and follow it, but do not do as they do, for they do not practice what they teach. The Pharisees' defect was their confusion in resting their security in their own genuine religious accomplishments, which had become the center of their lives. For example, I fast twice a week; I sit in the seat of honor; I am called rabbi, therefore, I am righteous. "Strikingly, Jesus indicted trusting in one's own 'success' as doing the will of God rather their security should rest solely in God, laying no claim to righteousness: 'God be merciful to me a sinner'" *(Jesus*

A New Vision). Unless your righteousness exceeds that of the scribes and Pharisees, you will never enter the kingdom of God—the fellowship of the righteous—a liberated Israel.

Foreword by Jaramogi: We seek to clarify what Christians are supposed to do in regards to faith and good works. A typical comment would be, "If I am not a do nothing Christian, I certainly am a do little Christian. My faith is accompanied by a few good works. I am dissatisfied with my life and the meaningless activities that fill my days. I am conscious of being lost even as I go through the motions of worship seeking the intervention of God. My family reflects my lost state with an aimless pattern of drifting. Neither my spouse nor my children have the slightest idea about where we are headed. We lie in the middle of the road torn between the values of two worlds. One is the world of the oppressor where we seek to find importance in a marriage, in a job, in attending college, but that world never gave us much value. Yet, we are lured by it because it offers material possessions that give us a shallow sense of importance. The other world is the Church-the Kingdom of God-the Black Nation, yet we don't find value there either because it stands opposed to the oppressor's world. We are not yet convinced that Nation building is God's will or that it gives us life and value. Even though we say we believe, our belief is not strong enough to motivate us to work sacrificially to build a New World." Little faith yields little work makes ***do little Christians***. So, in the middle of the road, it is difficult to give loyalty and commitment to anything. Our days are filled with this emptiness as it is with our spouse and our children.

Do Little Christians... Religion is Largely Empty Emotions

"We are lost on a merry-go-round of confusion." Religion for most is worship without substance, prayers without a God real enough to hear them, and fellowship without love" (Jaramogi). We go through the motions. We attend worship service, but don't really worship. Our minds are on other things, and our children are engaged in their own conversations. During our prayers, our minds are still pre-occupied with other thoughts, and the one praying seems to be preaching to the congregation rather than calling on a Power, which can hear and respond. The fellowship is perceived as **only** having a good time rather than loving one another. "Our righteousness must exceed that of the Pharisees." Religion by definition is "An organized system of beliefs and rituals centering upon God and pursued with zeal and devotion" (The American Heritage Dictionary). But ***do little Christians*** say, "I never thought that keeping my covenant promise with God is actually doing the will of God, nor did I think of God's promise in the covenant as conditional—conditional upon whether or not I actually do God's will. So, my salvation is conditional not unconditional upon whether I can make a connection between faith and good works in my life."

"When I am sick and death seems more than a distant bad dream, I sort of wish that my salvation was not quite so conditional and I began to think of good reasons for my lost state" (Jaramogi). "At the time of death, I face the stark reality that I have not done much with my life to evidence my faith, and that which has always been with me but which I ignored, the feeling that God has conditions and requirements. At the time of death, my prayer is please God forgive me!"

God Ought to Realize the Influences that Take My Mind off Salvation and Good Works

"Certainly the evils of the world are so overpowering that I can be excused for letting them blot out the presence of God and my need for His intervention" (Jaramogi). ***Do little Christians*** spin round and round on the merry-go-round of confusion. Some think God is cruel or He wouldn't allow poverty, wars, and diseases to run rampant. He wouldn't allow the evils of the world to be so pervasive. But, since He did, I find no logical rea-

son to call upon Him. Since He is the cause, I am sure He excuses me for the trouble I see. God knows why I drink so much. Or, I know God is understanding and merciful. He loves and forgives me all the time. Even though unemployment, health, and racism are grave issues facing Black people, and the problems exceed my ability to resolve them, I know God excuses me for taking my mind off salvation and good works. I am insecure about my job, about my spouse, about life in general, and I find very little time to work for God. I am sure he excuses me for blotting out His presence.

In addition to the distraction of evil in the world, there's the failure of the church to speak with one voice. The church speaks with many voices, and you have to choose which one you want. The many voices of the church add to the circle of confusion. Jesus said, *"Therefore, whoever breaks one of the least of these commandments, and teaches others to do the same will be called least in the kingdom of God."* Yet, some churches indirectly say it is okay to serve idols in the form of material possessions. From the pulpit of mega churches, God is the god who delivers idols of money, houses, and cars, while some say God abhors materialism. Some say you can go directly to God while others say you need an intermediary. Some say you go to purgatory or limbo after death, while others say it is either heaven or hell. Yet, others say

God calls you home at death, no matter what type of life you lived. Some say Jesus is the light of the world, but elevate Paul's individualistic salvation from the pulpit making it seem like he is the light of the world. Some preach only from the New Testament, saying it is the new covenant, and not much emphasis is put on the Old Testament. As a result, Christians think 100 different things a*nd we ride up and down, round and round on this confusion.*

In The Old Testament, Israel Constituted God's Chosen People. God Spoke To Israel. Everything Was Monitored By Rabbis and High Priests

We still have points of confusion. In the New Testament, John the Baptist came preaching a baptism of repentance. He baptized unto salvation that you are saved by the act of baptism. People went down into the river and rose in a newness of life. Yet, he sent his own disciples to question Jesus, *"Are thou the Messiah or do we wait for another?"* Jesus replied, *"Tell John what you see."* Jesus pointed to his good works. The Essenes separated themselves to establish transforming communities where their lives were monitored by the community, which transformed the believers. "The followers of Jesus and others were baptized into a transforming fellowship monitored by Jesus. After Pentecost, the Christian fellowship became a church as seen in the Book of Acts. The Essenes transforming community was added to the fellowship that Jesus established" (Jaramogi). How do we get off this merry-go-round of confusion, and re-order our lives on faith and good works? The answer lies in the Pan African Orthodox Christian Church.

The PAOCC brings all the trends of early tradition together. The PAOCC marks the end of being lost on the merry-go-round of confusion by offering a synthesis of all the religious trends leading up to Christianity, but members mess up and stay confused by accepting some and rejecting others. This is why we settle for *do little Christian* status. From Israel, we accept the New Jerusalem concept of Nation; from the Essenes, the transforming community of righteousness with structure and rules; from John the Baptist and Jesus, the baptism of repentance; from Jesus, emphasis on good works and love in a fellowship; from the disciples at Pentecost, the Holy Spirit—those who were touched went out to do good works (Jaramogi). In accepting and growing in the understanding of BCN theology, we gain clarity, and discover that we follow a legacy of struggle evidenced by faith and good works, and we are called by God, at this time in history, to do the same! Then, our righteousness will exceed that of the Pharisees!

THE INNER STRUGGLE

"From the moment of birth,
Each individual begins the difficult task
Of choosing which system he will permit
To dominate and control his life."

—Jaramogi

WAWA ABI:
Hardiness, toughness and perseverance

"Again, the devil took him to a very high mountain and showed him all the kingdoms of the world and their splendor; and he said to him, 'All these I will give you, if you will fall down and worship me.' Jesus said to him, away with you, Satan! For it is written, Worship the Lord your God, and serve only Him."

(Matthew 4:8-10)

Bible Lesson: About 2,000 years ago, the Black Nation Israel was oppressed by the white gentile Romans, who exploited them, persecuted them, and even put them to death for adhering to their covenant religion. Many of the Israelites accepted the values and lifestyle of their Roman oppressors, so their minds were warped. They, the oppressed, thought and behaved as the oppressors, but had no power. They, too, exploited their *own people.* They, too, condemned to death those with revolutionary zeal. They, too, grew in corruption and individualism. The evil, fragmented state of Israel inspired many to leave the corrupt cities, to set themselves apart, and to build communal and righteous communities committed to the will of God. These were the Essenes. Their way of life influenced God to act, to send Jesus, The Liberator—The Messiah, into the world to aid Israel in her troubles.

During Jesus' baptism in the River Jordan by John the Baptist, he was anointed with Godpower. "*And when Jesus had been baptized, just as he came up from the water, suddenly the heavens were opened to him and he saw the Spirit of God descending like a dove and alighting on him"* (Matthew 3:16). Then Jesus was led up by the Spirit into the wilderness to be tempted by the devil. It was here that he was engaged in an inner *struggle* to reject evil. In the first temptation, the tempter said, *"If you are the Son of God, command these stones to become loaves of bread"* (Matthew 4: 3). Jesus remembered the teachings of Moses (Deuteronomy 8:3), and rejected the temptation to use Godpower for selfish purposes. He said *"One does not live by bread alone, but by every word that comes from the mouth of God."* In other words, the power I have must be used for the will of God, not my own.

The devil tempted him the second time as he took Jesus to the holy city and placed him on the pinnacle of the temple. *"If you are the Son of God, throw yourself down."* Jesus rejected this temptation to test God, as he recalled again the teachings of Moses (Deuteronomy 6:16). Again, it is written, *"Do not put the Lord your God to the test."* In other words, who am I to test God to see what He will do. I am the one that needs testing, so God can see if I am committed to doing His will.

The devil tempted Jesus the third time showing him all the kingdoms of the world, and telling him, *"If you bow down and worship me, all these I will give you."* Jesus again recalled the law (Deuteronomy 6:13) and said,

"Away with you, Satan! For it is written, Worship the Lord your God and serve only Him." In other words, I reject the glories, prestige, and material possessions of a world controlled by Satan. If I accept this offer, in fact, I would also be serving Satan. I will worship the Lord, and serve Him only. *"Having exhausted all these ways of tempting him, the devil left him, to return at the appointed time."* Jesus, with the power of the Spirit, returned to Galilee.

> *"...And that the whole world lies under the power of the evil one."* (1 John 5:19)

"The Black Man's Search for God is an Inner Struggle to Reject the Evil, Secular Culture and to Establish a World Order in Which the Will of God is Supreme"

Jaramogi teaches that, "Two contradictory systems, representing good and evil, God and Satan, are constantly at war in the world seeking dominance and control." *God is the Unified Energy Field of Power;* the energy does not act in terms of good or evil, but can be manipulated by good and evil. The Divine System emanates from God, Cosmic Energy and Creative Intelligence. We are seldom aware of it because our rational mind limits us. So, we must be engaged in processes (communal living, devotionals, rituals, and worship) that break through these limitations, in order to experience God, and to experience a higher consciousness. This state of enlightenment makes us aware of the love, the harmony, the unity and balance that exist in the divine system, and how communalism is the highest expression of this system.

The world system is Satan personified for it accepts the concept of individualism. It is not characterized by love, harmony, unity and balance as the Divine System, but by selfishness, hatred, greed, isolation, violence, war, unfaithfulness, deceit, theft, dishonesty, injustice, and oppression. It is in disobedience to God.

"From the moment of birth, each individual begins the difficult task of choosing which system he will permit to dominate and control his life". (Jaramogi) Sadly, before a child turns one year old, he has been trained by individualistic parents to accept an evil, secular culture. He is exposed to bouts of individualism between the parents; he listens to the conversation between adults and picks up the negative energy; he observes the facial expressions and body language of those around him and mimics them. Parents allow their children to hit and throw tantrums. They do not set any boundaries to this behavior because they are too small or too cute. We groom our children to worship Satan. Each one of us must decide whom we shall serve—God or Satan.

"To Make No Conscious Choice, Rejecting Evil and Embracing Good, Means that Evil will Triumph by Default"

Do not be deceived! People make the statement, "If I am not harming anyone, then anything I do is all right." We eloquently rationalize why we have made no conscious choice to reject evil and embrace good. "I am not a murderer, only a liar; therefore, I am not evil. I am not a liar, only dishonest; therefore, I am not evil. I am not an adulterer, only a player; therefore, I am not evil. I am not a selfish person, only a hateful one; therefore, I am not evil. I am not a hypocrite; I am just individualistic sometimes; therefore, I am not evil. I am not that bad actually, I just do not believe in giving total commitment to the Church; therefore, I am not evil. Do not be deceived! Evil is evil! Unless we make a conscious choice rejecting evil and embracing good, we will automatically act in an evil manner, because our individualism will prevail. *"But one is tempted by one's own desire, being lured and enticed by it; then, when that desire has conceived, it gives birth to sin"* (James 1:15).

"Individualism (selfish desires are more important than the needs and goals of a group), and hedonism (the doctrine that only that which is pleasurable is good) are as natural as breathing to a newborn child, and unless deliberately checked will lead inescapably to the

acceptance of evil as a way of life" (Jaramogi). We selectively dabble in an evil world, and choose what we want or what brings us pleasure. In our compromise with Satan, we allow our children to do the same, so that by the time they reach the age of twelve, the Church and its leadership are viewed as having no authority. No compromise can be made if we and our children are to be saved from evil. *"Sin, when it is fully grown gives birth to death"* (James 1:16). We must reject evil as Jesus did. *"Worship the Lord your God, and serve Him only."*

"Only the Practice of Communalism can Check our Free Fall into a World of Evil."

"We are forced then to decide what to believe about authority, rewards and punishment, God, heaven, and hell." (Jaramogi) Do we accept the authority of the Pan African Orthodox Christian Church to speak and act for God? Do we accept the law and the prophets as God's revelations to man? Do we believe our rewards are blessings of health, happiness, and collective prosperity experienced only through communal living? Do we believe that in choosing evil, we build a hell on earth, and our punishment will be suffering and death? Do we believe our souls will go to hell after death if we choose evil during life?

Like Jesus, we should all reject the secular culture of the devil and work to build a counter culture where God is the focus, and the authority. This first requires participation with a group of people who are sincerely engaged in *fighting* the corruption within themselves. Each group meeting must involve a discussion of what we have been called to do as outlined in the sermon, the bible class, and orientation lecture. Then, the group must be led to encounter, where members can honestly speak about behaviors which work against the goals of the group, and which violate our covenant relationship with God. Individualistic behaviors cannot be overlooked. The group's participation in maintaining the covenant vows of community outreach, missionary outreach, Kodi, Expansion, Beulah Land, and accountability must be evaluated. This checks our free fall into a world of evil.

The Church provides its members with attractive opportunities to work together for the accomplishment of common goals compatible with covenant vows, and the revolutionary struggle in the liberation of Black people. Devotionals, *prayer, meditation,* rituals and worship allow *us to communicate with God as energy* beings. Kazi, youth work, post assignments, dining hall, training center clean-up assignments, and choir are all opportunities for us to work together to build a righteous and communal nation. It is by our rejection of an evil, secular culture of the devil, by our commitment to uphold covenant vows, and by our work that we *"Worship the Lord our God, and serve only Him."*

THE BLACK MAN'S SEARCH FOR GOD

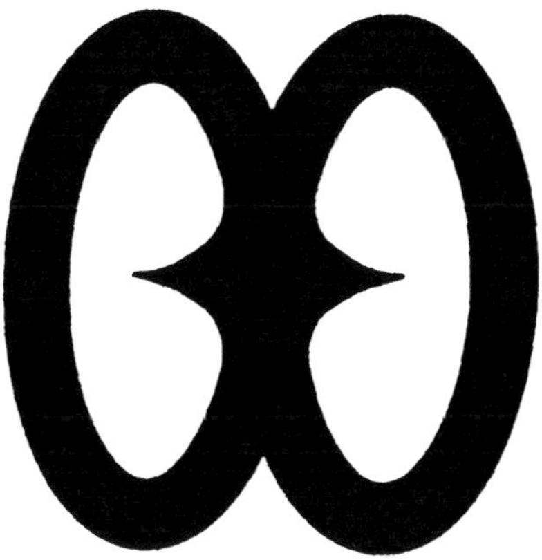

"Our prayers and petitions must conceive of one GOD able to communicate with all people everywhere—simultaneously—and able to transform everything in the cosmos at will."

—Jaramogi

NYAME BIRIBI WO SORO: Hope and Inspiration
GOD, there is something in the heavens!

"When you have had children and children's children, and become complacent in the land, if you act corruptly by making an idol in the form of anything, thus doing what is evil in the sight of the Lord your God, and provoking him to anger, I call heaven and earth to witness against you today that you will soon utterly perish from the land that you are crossing the Jordan to occupy; you will not live long on it, but will be utterly destroyed. The Lord will scatter you among the peoples....There you will serve other gods. From there you will seek the Lord your God, and you will find Him if you search after Him with all your heart and soul."

(Deuteronomy 4:25-29)

Bible Lesson: "Deuteronomy is a farewell address by Moses." *(Interpreter's Dictionary)* He reminds the Black Nation Israel that they have a relationship with God; the God of Israel was conceived as a powerful personality...a super being. He tells Israel that they are about to enter the Promised Land, and recalls their experiences. He reminds them of the time God instructed him to appoint tribal leaders; *"I am unable by myself to bear you... choose for each of your tribes individuals who are wise and reputable to be your leaders"* (Deuteronomy 1:9-13). He continues with how they refused to enter the Promised Land before because they were unwilling and afraid, and how the Lord punished them for rebelling against His will by sending them back into the wilderness until the old generation died off. *"Just as soon as all the warriors had died off from among the people, the Lord spoke to me for us to cross the boundary of Moab"* (Deuteronomy 2:16). The Lord was with us as we defeated the Kings of Sihon and Og. Now as you are about to enter the land sworn to our ancestors, you must be obedient to God. Moses warns them that they will be utterly destroyed as a nation if they become complacent in the land, forgetting that they have a Covenant relationship with God and covenant vows to fulfill. They will be scattered among other nations as a powerless people if they accept other gods. *"There you will serve other gods made by human hands"* (Deuteronomy 4:28). "When you experience the suffering and distress of being oppressed, and the misery of not being a people, you will return to the Lord your God and heed Him. *Seek the Lord,* Moses urges them. *"Follow the commandments, and obey the Law, which hold you together as a people. You will find God and He will protect you and bless you if you search after Him with all your heart and soul."*

Introduction: *"We are dealing with the Black man's search for God. When we first came into The Pan African Orthodox Christian Church (PAOCC), we attempted to discard the God of our white oppressor. We tried to revere the* *ancient gods of Africa who revealed themselves to our ancestors eons before any attempt was made by God to communicate with the more primitive people who had broken away from the African continent."*

–Jaramogi

"Today, in the PAOCC, we conceive of God as Cosmic Energy and Creative Intelligence. This is not the God of our African ancestors; nor is it the God of our white oppressors."

The unification theory is expressed today by physicists who state that the universe has four forces. "There's gravity, electromagnetism, (a combination of two forces, electricity and magnetism), the nuclear strong force and the nuclear weak force" (*Houston Chronicle Magazine*). At high energy levels, these forces merge into one force. The forces are unified. Jaramogi teaches us that the "oppressor's concept of science is closer to the PAOCC's conception of the Black man's God than the white man's conception of God." In our church, we conceive of God as Cosmic Energy and Creative Intelligence...the powerful and intelligent Unified Energy Field in which we live, move, and have our being.

We revere the gods of our ancestors because they indicate that African people had a spiritual awareness and religious life a long time before others. Our ancestors believed that the gods were "spirit beings" that blessed and protected them; the sky goddess, the air-god, the earth-god and others were only a few. Later, these ancient gods traveled with people of Africa as they were dispersed as slaves throughout the world, taking bits and pieces of their revelations with them, but never comprehending the basic unification of all Cosmic Energy and Creative Intelligence into one God. The belief in the ancient gods traveled with the slave ships to the cane fields of the Caribbean, to the slums of Brazil, and to the cotton fields and ghettos of America. Everywhere the slave ships stopped, the revelations of the African gods were mixed with the teachings of the Roman Catholic and Protestant Churches making a hybrid religion; Voodoo, Santeria of Cuba, and the Macumba of *Brazil. "Our gods come from Africa. Our slave ancestors were also from Africa. Africa is the land of life"* (*Macumba*, pg. 35).

Our oppressor's concept of God was derived from Israel's belief of God as one super being. In fact, the God of ancient Africa is known elsewhere by other names. However, Europeans, in trying to define Jesus, included him as God in the flesh who bears our sins so that upon personal acceptance of him we may go to heaven after death. These are the teachings of the Roman Catholic and Protestant Churches derived from the Apostle Paul's doctrine of individual salvation ... a distortion of Christianity, which opposes the communal, revolutionary *mission* of the Black Messiah, Jesus. The PAOCC's concept of God is not the same as our ancestors or our white oppressors.

"As we prepare to enter the New Millennium, we must undertake to reorganize our total theology to conform to our new conception of God."

The cultural life of Africa, including the religion of the African gods were disrupted, distorted, and destroyed by the invasion of the white European barbarians who, with military power made possible by the use of gunpowder and firearms, were able to invade, conquer, and enslave; thereby destroying life on the continent by war and conflict. The Africans were systematically robbed of their culture and civilization, and plugged into a way of life, which deliberately kept them ignorant and helpless for generations. The religion of Israel was preserved and given to the slaves in the Old Testament teachings of Christianity. The slaves identified with these because of Israel's Egyptian bondage and her liberation struggle under Moses. The old spirituals express this: *"O Mary don't you weep. Tell Martha not* to *moan. Pharaoh's* ar*my died in the Red Sea, O Mary don't you weep. Tell Martha not to moan."* The slaves received the Paulinian individualistic theology of the

Roman Catholic and Protestant Churches, and the liberation theology of Israel, which made of this strange combination, a powerful evangelical communal mix that guided the slave through the difficult years of slavery. "*Yes, we all shall be free. Yes, we all shall be free.* Yes, *we all shall be free, when the Lord shall appear.*"

Today, hundreds of years later, even though we cast off most of the physical shackles, which masked our slavery, we are still enslaved by the cultural, psychological, and educational remnants of our enslavement. We are the slaves of our own memory. Our home training, our church training, and our work training are similar to the ways we learned during slavery. In a slave master's sermon, he says to his slaves, "Servants, obey your master according to the flesh. It is your duty to rise promptly in the morning at the blowing of the horn. The bible says too much sleep is not good for either the body or mind, If you yield to a little more sleep, you sin, and you will burn forever in hell. God wants you to work all day and most of the night for your master who suffers from bronchitis." Black preachers today preach, "Love your enemy—you do not have to do anything, God will deliver you. Let us pray that God will change the conscious of the white man so he will accept us. God will take me up to heaven; I pray that you will get there too."

Even though we now define God as Cosmic Energy and Creative Intelligence, the Unified Energy Field, we still think in terms of the simpler more primitive theology of Israel. We must discard the personal god of Israel as well as the individualistic god of Apostle Paul.

"Our prayers and petitions must conceive of one God able to communicate with all people everywhere—simultaneously—and able to transform everything in the cosmos at will."

We are Black, oppressed and about to enter a new *millennium* where our survival is questionable. As the world becomes highly technological in which science and mathematical skills are crucial, our oppressor's system of benign neglect is deliberately designed so that we become obsolete. This can be seen in our mis-education, unemployment, and the mounting deterioration of Black neighborhoods. We receive little or no assistance in funds or resources from the federal government, state or local government. The forces working against us are great and our primitive concept of God places limitations on what "He" can do to help us.

Today, in the PAOCC, we conceive of God as the Unified Energy Field combining all the energy in the cosmos with Creative Intelligence and the ability to communicate with billions of people simultaneously. We know that the Pentium II computer chip can process 500 million instructions every second; therefore, this new conception does not limit God. What it does is expand our ability to comprehend the infinite power God has at "His" disposal, and the limitless responses "He" can make for our prayers and petitions. God heard the cries of the Black Nation Israel through their suffering in Israel, and responded by sending Moses into Egypt as the liberator. God felt the remorse of the Essenes on behalf of Israel, as they prayed for intervention and set up righteous communities in which the people recommitted their lives. God responded and sent the Messiah Jesus to liberate the people. When the people rejected and crucified Jesus, the disciples reunited, remembered him and sought the Holy Spirit, who had empowered Jesus' life. At Pentecost, God sent the Holy Spirit, anointing them with the same messianic power bestowed upon Jesus at his baptism. The disciples set up the church in the Acts of the Apostles as the Messianic Community replacing the crucified Messiah. God has the power of limitless responses.

Our prayers and petitions to God, the Unified Energy Field, can be heard because we are energy beings and our emanations can influence God to respond in whatever way that "He" chooses. This concept of God deepens our faith that God is all-powerful, and through His Power, all things are possible.

Let us move from complacency. Let not heaven and earth witness against us. Let us not be scattered among the peoples, but distinguish ourselves as God's chosen people. Let us not serve our oppressor's God, which has no power to help us in our earthly oppression. Rather, let us seek the God of Cosmic Energy and Creative Intelligence. For the words of Moses still stand true today. *"From there you will seek the Lord your God, and you will find Him if you search after Him with all your heart and soul. He will not forget the covenant."*

KUA is the path we travel to find God.

OPENING OUR ENERGY CHANNELS

"The science of KUA helps us open ourselves to GOD. We feel cosmic energy flood our being. We close our eyes, and we can hear the drums of GOD."

—Jaramogi

GYE NYAME: Omnipotence, omnipresence, and immortality of GOD

> *"Ask, and it will be given you; search, and you will find; knock, and the door will be opened for you. For everyone who asks receives, and everyone who searches finds, and for everyone who knocks, the door will be opened."*
> (Matthew 7:7-8)

Bible Lesson: An invisible God or the "world of Spirit" is not part of Western worldview, but was the reality and common property of every culture prior to Western culture. This holds true for Judaism, an African religion. "At the heart of the Jewish tradition, indeed constituting it, was Israel's story of the intersection between the world of spirit and the world of ordinary experiences. The Hebrew Bible is Israel's story of events which were seen as disclosures of Spirit, of people who were experienced as mediators of Spirit, of laws and prophetic utterances which were believed to have been given by the Spirit" *(Jesus A New Vision).* Seeking a relationship with God was basic to the Jewish religion and evidenced by their Covenant relationship with God. They believed that a relationship with God would bring well being. *"The Lord is faithful in all His words, and gracious in all His deeds. The Lord upholds all who are falling, and raises up all who are bowed down. The eyes of all look to You, and You give them their food in due season. You open* *your hand, satisfying the desire of every living thing*" (Psalms 145: 13-16).

Jesus, in the tradition of the prophets and the Essenes, sought a relationship with God. He experienced God as Cosmic Energy and Creative Intelligence when John the Baptist baptized him in the River Jordan. He maintained a relationship with God as he carried out God's will of revolutionary transformation for his people. He healed the sick by laying on of hands, which realigned their energy flow. Jesus taught the spiritual reality of God which helped to sharpen their perceptions of who they were. He reassured them that a relationship with God was necessary for their salvation and well being. *"Ask, and it shall be given to you."* Petition God through prayer and worship, and God will answer. *"Seek, and you will find."* Quest for God and you will find happiness, and prosperity. *"Knock, and the door will be opened."* God is waiting right here. Just knock, and you will find God through the opened door. *"God will give good things to those who ask Him"* (Matthew 7:ll).

Foreword by Jaramogi: Our health and well being depend in large measure upon our relationship with God. Health is defined as *'the state of perfect physical, mental, social well being and spiritual well being...a state in which a person feels at every moment of living a joy and zest for life, a sense of fulfillment, and an awareness of harmony with the* *universe around him.*" (*Creating Health*, Chopra) God is the Great Energy Field in which we live, move, and have our being. God is everywhere. God is all around us.

Being created out of the substance of God, we are energy beings. The beat of our heart, the flow of our blood, the electrical impulses of our nerves, the movement of our muscles, the functioning of our internal organs, are all manifestations of an invisible energy force at work. Our health depends on the flow of energy and on how we function in this Great *Energy Field.*

Our problem in the Church and Christian life is to be able to function in the Great Energy Field. When we have closed ourselves off from God and the inflow of Cosmic Energy, we experience a deterioration of the physical body. There is an optimum, way to live. In Africa, people lived a life more compatible with the environment. When this way of life was disrupted, we never got ourselves together. It is very improbable that we could live harmonious lives in Africa after being disrupted by the white man.

To restore health and vitality, we have but to open our energy channels to find God at the door waiting...KUGASANA! To experience God in KUGASANA prepares spirit, mind, and body to do the will of God as required by our Covenant vows. God can provide everything necessary for health, happiness, and prosperity if we maintain a proper relationship with God.

> *God is Cosmic Energy and Creative Intelligence, the invisible Unified Energy Field...so religion deals "with energy and power."*
>
> —Jaramogi

We Can Open our Energy Channels With Prayer and Meditation

"Ask, and it will be given you." To open our energy channels, we must accept the reality of God as Cosmic Energy and Creative Intelligence. The concept of a personified God, a super man in the clouds, is not only untrue, but diminishes the possibility of a fulfilling life. God created us with energy channels so we could receive the flow of energy necessary to sustain life in our physical bodies. These energy channels must remain open for health and vitality if we are to receive the life force in abundance. We can open them with prayer and meditation. Jaramogi defines both as being in communion with God. *"Verbal prayer is only one form of prayer in the Jewish-Christian tradition. Indeed, it is only the first stage of prayer; internal silence and lengthy periods of time characterize deeper levels of*

prayer. In this state, one enters into deeper levels of consciousness; ordinary consciousness is stilled, and one sits quietly in the presence of God" (Jesus A New Vision). Random, busy, and endless thoughts bombard our minds each moment of the day and even well into the evening as we toss restlessly in our beds. Many of us find it difficult to keep still. We are addicted to "always doing something." Prayer and meditation alter our state of consciousness by stilling the thoughts and quieting the body. We are in a state of solitude. *"Be still and know that I am God"* (Psalms 46:10).

The worship services of the Church are designed to stimulate the free flow of energy within the body. Our service is divided into four distinct steps:

1. **Invocation/Meditation.** We invoke the presence of God, seeking to obtain a higher level of consciousness to open ourselves to the experience of God;

2. **Confession of Faith and Collective Petition.** We profess what we believe and collectively petition together to ask God to do the things that we need to have done (Creed, Anthem for the Black Nation, Responsive Meditation);

3. **Sacrament of Commitment.** We renew our Covenant relationship with God and renew our communal relationships with one another;

4. **Sermon.** We seek to hear the will of God...it convicts us of sin and is a warning against the world system. Members participating sincerely in worship can collectively raise the energy level making a path for the experience of God.

We can open our energy channels with group encounters, which help remove blocks such as guilt, acceptance of the myth of black inferiority (ABI), and mixed up personal relationships.

"Seek and you will find." Our experiences of being brutally uprooted from our Motherland and of worldwide injustices resulted in the destruction of the Black man's spirit/mind/body integration by creating energy blocks. We are plagued with guilt about most things; the way we ended a personal relationship, the way we raised our children, not meeting the expectations of our parents, not living up to our oppressor's standards, and hurting someone verbally or physically. We are guilt ridden. We accept the myth of Black inferiority ...a belief that my people and I are inferior. This feeling is repressed, but shows itself in gossip, in

demeaning conversations, in low expectations, in lack of study and vision, in low productivity, and a disregard for Black authority. All these are based on feelings of personal inadequacy. Our relationships are a source of chaos and conflict. Each individual, feeling inadequate and insecure, is busy manipulating for control through verbal and oftentimes physical abuse. Fights and disagreements arise. We can't understand each other. We take everything personally.

The group encounters offer an environment in which the individual can honestly disclose his feelings of inadequacy and problems in personal relationships releasing his guilt feelings. Members can discuss the effects of their behaviors upon others. This is done in the context of a willingness to uphold the Covenant and to fulfill the goals of the group. In the fulfillment of group goals, members realize that they can do more than what they thought, thus eroding the blocks of the acceptance of black inferiority. It is in the encounter where members become aware that we must move from individualism to communalism; our willingness to change motivates us to learn to function within a group, thus eroding the block of individualism. An effective encounter leaves members with a real experience of relief and oneness because the mental energy blocks have been removed.

We can open our energy channels with group disciplines; Tai Chi, Yoga, massage and KUA group devotionals.

"Knock and the door will be opened for you." The ancient disciplines of Tai Chi and Yoga open energy channels through movements. These movements are not done alone during ordinary daily activities, but together, in a group. This allows each group member to "suspend his/her will"...altering the state of consciousness. The collective breathing and group movements open the energy channels of the body. The ancient technique of massage, through touch, stimulates the muscles, tissues and organs—melting away blocks of tension. KUA small group devotionals are a total worship experience involving the four steps of the worship service, and all the disciplines. *"Group disciplines help break down the barriers of individualism preparing the body to do good works and allowing you to have wholesome relationships with other people."* All of these allow us to have a relationship with God...with energy and power. Health, vitality, an openness to others, and power to struggle are real experiences which give fulfillment of life. The PAOCC is the culmination of the religion of our ancestors, and the true practitioner of Christianity. Everything we need is available for us. If we would just seek, we will find!

UTILIZING THE CREATIVE ENERGY OF GOD

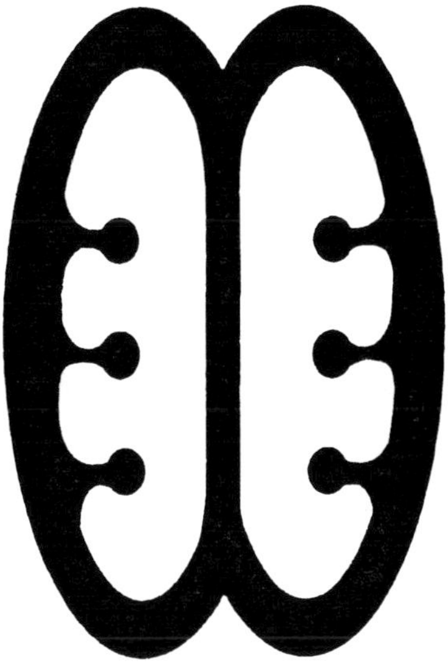

"The essences of all being is energy. The Church seeks to utilize this energy system upon which life depends by bringing together a fellowship of persons who practice disciplines, rituals, and sacraments, which 'open' the individual for both the Experience of God and the Experience of Community."

—Jaramogi

ESE NE TEKREMA: Improvement, advancement, growth, the need for friendliness and interdependence

"In the beginning, God created the heavens and earth, the earth was a formless void and darkness covered the face of the deep, while a wind from God swept over the face of the waters."
(Genesis 1:1-2)

Bible Lesson: In the beginning, a cosmic explosion occurred at creation, and the universe came into being making everything an expression and outgrowth of the energy of God (Cosmic Energy and Creative Intelligence). This belief in the transcedent reality is called Pantheism and was shared by many. However, the experiences of the Kung Tribe indicate an inner power. The book, *Boiling Energy*, written about the healing energy of the Kung Tribe of the Kalahari Desert in southern Africa, documents their experiences of being conduits for healing. Kia is an altered state of consciousness. Num is energy. *"The singing and dancing at the main fire continue, the voices enthusiastic, the songs growing in rhythm and volume as each nears its end. Bau's singing is strong; her head lifts up, her mouth pointing to the sky. Her mood is intense, her eyes mainly closed, she moves with the music, talking little. Now, still singing strongly, she starts to sway. She falls over; completely limp, into the arms of the singer who sits next to her. She moans softly and begins to gasp for breath. Bau has* *entered Kia. She is healing each woman in the singing circle."*

> *In the Pan African Orthodox Christian Church, we now have to focus on a transition from the idea of Pantheism to the concept of each individual having an energy system."*
>
> —Jaramogi

We Are Energy Beings in an Energy Cosmos with All Our Relationships Being Energy Relationships

Each individual, being an outgrowth and expression of the energy of God, is an energy being with an energy system. This system is composed of chakras (energy centers) through which cosmic energy flows. The Path of Cosmic Energy flows through the seven energy centers, and activates Kundalini, a dormant or static cosmic energy located at the base of the spine. When the centers are blocked, cosmic energy cannot flow freely and poor health results.

All of our relationships are energy relationships, which means there is an exchange of energy between individuals. However, our association with other beings and our relationships depend on our state of mind. "Our state of mind is a problem"(Jaramogi). Blocks exist because of "negative emotions (anger, fear, self-criticism, guilt, greed, resentment), psychological stress (family problems, tensions at work, loss of money or job, divorce, death in the family), lethargy (mental inertia), and unwholesome surroundings, contact with other people's negativity, and violent, crude, or shocking books or other forms of entertainment" (*Perfect Health*, Chopra, 1991). In The Pan African Orthodox Christian Church, the Sacraments, bible class, worship, devotionals, and rituals are designed to change the state of mind in order to remove the blocks. Participation in these allows us to rise above wrong thinking. Another important quality that helps us to change is the anticipation of transformation.

This "looking forward to" that something can and will happen is essential to change. This feeling must be a part of early training in each of us. The KUA workshop (a session utilizing chanting, awareness, yoga, Tai Chi, and meditation to open a person to God) is designed to add to a person's anticipation. All of these prepare us for the opening (Kugasana) and train us to be Christians. When a group of people come together in faith, and expect something to happen, they activate the adrenaline flow within the body. The adrenaline "prepares the organism for emotional stress (fight or flight) by increasing blood pressure and blood sugar level, and by widening air passages in the lungs. With the adrenaline flow, the anticipation increases, the energy rises and has an effect in what we are doing...it is this boiling energy that can heal/transform".

Building A Nation Requires the Creative Energy of God

The Bible is evidence of the Creative Energy of God in nation building as shown in the history of the Black Nation Israel. In order to build a nation, people are needed. "God created male and female..." (Genesis 26: 27). A nation stands under the judgment of God and God responds to evil and sin. The Flood reflects this. "The Lord saw that the wickedness of humankind was great in the earth ... So the Lord said, 'I will blot out from the earth the human beings I have created...I will send rain on the earth and every living thing that I have made I will blot out from the face of the earth'" (Genesis 6:5,7). God expects humankind to maintain the Covenant from generation to generation. "This is My covenant, which you shall keep, between Me and you and your offspring after you: Every male among you shall be circumcised" (Genesis 17:10). God destroys Sodom for its wickedness. "Then the Lord rained on Sodom and Gomorrah sulfur and fire from the Lord out of heaven" (Genesis 19:24). God helps Esau and Jacob to reconcile. "Jacob said, 'No, please; if I find favor with you, then accept my present from my hand; for truly to see your face is like seeing the face of God—since you have received me with such favor" (Genesis 33:10). God sends plagues upon Egypt so Pharaoh would let His people go. "Then the Lord said to Moses, 'Go to Pharaoh and say to him, Thus says the Lord: Let My people go, so that they may worship me. If you refuse to let them go, I will plague your whole country with frogs" (Exodus 8:1-2). "God assisted with each incident. This was the creative energy of God working in the world. The problem is that God could do anything and Black people today would not give God any credit." (Jaramogi)

Working With God's Energy Today Is Our Salvation

With God's energy, we can remove blocks and establish a free flow of energy, which makes life a celebration where we enjoy health, happiness, prosperity, and freedom. The PAOCC offers psychohistory and the disciplines of meditation, prayer, and Yoga to help us focus on the spiritual environment rather than on self. Working with God's energy, we can raise our energy to a boiling point. God has revealed to us the Science of KUA and because of God, we are blessed with an environment where Kugasana (Experience of God) can come when we look forward with great expectation that something will and can happen. When we activate our own energy within the group, we raise the energy level to a boiling point. This boiling energy can heal our state of mind, can heal our sick, and our suffering. We then have clarity of mind to focus our energy on solving the many problems that face us as a people. As it did with the Black Nation Israel, God's energy will help us build a Nation for our people.

THE COVENANT FAITH

"Created out of the very substance of GOD, we have come together in the Transforming Community where the power of GOD is..."

—Jaramogi

NSOROMA: Faith and the belief in patronage and dependency of a Supreme Being
A child of the heavens.

"It was because the Lord loved you and kept the oath that He swore to your ancestors, that the Lord has brought you out with a mighty hand, and redeemed you from the house of slavery, from the hand of Pharaoh king of Egypt. Know therefore that the Lord your God is God, the faithful God who maintains covenant loyalty with those who love Him and keep His commandments, to a thousand generations."
(Deuteronomy 7: 8-9)

Bible Lesson: The faith of the Black Nation Israel was centered on the covenant God made with Abraham and his sons into perpetuity for a thousand generations; *"I'll be your God if you will be My people.* "This covenant required that Israel maintain a relationship with God, as stated in the first commandment. "You *shall have no other gods before Me. You shall not make for yourself an idol, whether in the form of anything that is in heaven above, or that is on the earth beneath, or that is in the water under the earth* " (Genesis 5: 6-8), "I *am the Lord your God."*

At this time in Israel's history, they were preparing to enter the land God had promised them. Moses would not enter the Promised Land, and in his farewell address spoke to the people of Israel reminding them who they were, what God had done for them, and what they had to do to maintain their covenant relationship with God.

He talks to them to make them conscious of identifying with each other as God's people. *"For you are a people holy to the Lord your God; the Lord your God has chosen you out of all the peoples on earth to be His people, His treasured possession"* (Genesis 7:6). Moses recalls what God had done in order to strengthen their faith in God's miraculous power. The Lord brought you out of Egypt, freed you from slavery, fed you manna, and quenched your thirst in the wilderness.

Moses strictly warns them of what they must do to remain a unified people for he is aware of the Canaanite worship of Baal, and the tendency of the Israelites to do the same. *"Make no covenant with the nations you will defeat; do not intermarry with them, for that would turn away your children from following Me, to serve other gods. Break down their altars, and burn their idols."*

He implores them to keep God's commandments, their covenant vows, and if they do, God would remain faithful, loving them, blessing them, and multiplying them. Their children would be blessed, their crop plentiful, their cattle and the issue of flock would increase, and all diseases turned away. Moses teaches them that they have a relationship with God as a people, and upon this basis the power of God can be focused on their behalf.

Foreword by Jaramogi: When we enter any building that has been consecrated for its sacred use, we are conscious of the invisible power that gives the church its reason for being. Even without entering the building, the steeple with its cross pointed towards the heaven gives a sense of awe for the invisible Godpower which is present; even when the symbol is a humble storefront with a painted sign on the window announcing its consecration, or an altar with a bible and candle, or a sincere believer making the sign of the cross to acknowledge the Holy. All of these symbols represent and acknowledge Godpower. The church only exists because it stands for the miraculous—Godpower in everyday life.

When We Once Experience and Acknowledge Our Relationship with God, We Become Seekers, and Try to Recapture that Miraculous Godpower that has Touched and Transformed Our Lives

"It was because the Lord loved you..."

Godpower worked miracles on Israel's behalf with the plagues against Egypt, the parting of the Red Sea, the pillar of cloud in the day and the pillar of fire at night which led Israel out of Egypt, and many more.

When we experience and acknowledge our relationship with God, we become seekers.

Can you recall the time when you became aware of how dissatisfied you were with life, and how you sought happiness in all the wrong places? Can you remember how you felt the first time you came upon the truth regarding Black people, and how it touched you very deeply? Do you remember making the decision to visit the Shrine, and your experience when you joined? It was as if you were lifted up in ecstasy experiencing the energy all around you, and feeling like you had made it home. That was Godpower touching and transforming your life. You have not been the same since then! Acknowledging God has led you and touched you making you a seeker wherein you try to recapture that miraculous Godpower again.

However, the crux of our modern dilemma is to believe or not to believe in a miraculous experience. Did it happen or are we only confused? We also face the question of, "Can we make our experience of Godpower compatible with the science that we have been taught or think we have been taught?" (Jaramogi), Science, in the past, has been taught on a physical cause and effect level; what the eye can see. It gave little regard to the invisible activity and reactions taking place in all life. *"For the scientist who has lived by his faith in the power of reason, the story ends like a bad dream. He has scaled the mountains of ignorance; he is about to conquer the highest peak; as he pulls himself over the final rock, he is greeted by a band of theologians who have been sitting there for centuries"* (Silk, 1992).

The New Scientific Conception of Power Consisting of the Unified Energy Field, which Brings Together All Energy and Power in The Cosmos is Much the Same as the New Religious Conception of God as the Unification of Cosmic Energy and Creative Intelligence

"Know therefore that the
Lord your God is God..."

The "Grand Unification Theory" of the new scientists is that four fundamental forces of the universe are united and inter-related. The forces are gravity, electromagnetic, and two sub-atomic forces (one strong and one weak). These forces consist of the same energy "particles", but they cannot be seen. They move at various speeds (very rapid or slow), some repelling and attracting, some exchanging electrical charges, some exchanging color; their very activity is power. These forces permeate the whole universe including every living and non-living entity. The universe is controlled by this invisible power. (Trefil, 1983).

Our Holy Patriarch, Jaramogi Abebe Agyeman, teaches that "All energy is *unified* in a single energy field which is God." The new science conception of the grand unification of energy and the new religion conception of God being the Unified Energy Field are much the same. "This new awareness of a single energy binding together all aspects of the cosmos, traditional contradictions between science and religion disappear, and there is no scientific reason why religious miracles cannot take place as recounted in the bible, and in the daily experiences of Covenant Christians."

The Unified Energy Field (God) which brings together all energy has the ability to FOCUS this limitless power in anyway compatible with the revealed will of God expressed by the Law and the prophets, and with God's covenant promise to do for man whatever they ask if they are obedient to His revealed will. The Law (10 Commandments) demands that Israel reject individualism: Thou shall not kill, not steal, not lie, and not covet thy neighbor's wife or property. The prophets spoke of communalism declaring that the people were responsible for one another by caring for the poor, the orphan and the widow. They reminded the people of the Law so they could maintain their covenant relationship with God. If they did this, Godpower would be focused on them, as a people, healing them, protecting them, and blessing them.

As a Christian, Your Access to Godpower Depends Upon the Group to Which You are a Part as the People of God

"He is the faithful God who maintains covenant loyalty with those who love Him and keep His commandments."

Godpower is not accessed by individual requests because God's will is that you belong to a covenant group. What you pray for must be compatible with what the group needs! Many of us do not really believe this, so we end up blocking the prayers of group members, and blocking God's response. When we don't identify or participate in the group, we are "shut down," too weak to send waves of energy into the Unified Energy Field, and too blocked to receive them. Jaramogi teaches: "That if you wonder why God does not hear your cries for help and answers your prayers is simply because:

1. You do not accept the covenant faith enjoined by God by honoring the covenant vows you are required to accept by being God's people;

2. You do not accept communalism as God's way of life for His people; and

3. You have not become one of the people of God by joining a covenant church (group).

As members of the Pan African Orthodox Christian Church, we accept the covenant which makes us the people of God, joined together communally in His Church. As the people of God, we are required to obey His will as revealed by the Law and the prophets. Our covenant vows require us to reject individualism and accept communalism as God's way of life. So, the church and the covenant are important because by our participation, we inherit the promises of God. Without it, we have no promise of Godpower being available to us to help us confront the problems in everyday life.

We acknowledge our acceptance of the covenant in which God responds to our prayers as the People of God (group). It is our collective righteousness that opens the community to receive Godpower; the group is your only access to it. You cannot resolve your problems by yourself. You cannot build a better world for your children by yourself. You need the spiritual support of the People of God. Together with them, your spiritual power can touch God, and God will respond. Our Covenant Faith opens us to miracles!

MAINTAINING A COMPATIBLE RELATIONSHIP WITH GOD

"We must learn to belong. This is the Group Experience. The Group tears down the walls of individualism. Socialization is necessary before the individual can seek the Experience of GOD!"

—Jaramogi

BINKABI: Justice, fairplay, freedom, peace, forgiveness, unity, harmony, and the avoidance of conflicts or strife

No one should bite another, outrage or provoke another

> *"Because you did not serve the Lord your God joyfully and with gladness of heart for the abundance of everything, therefore you shall serve your enemies whom the Lord will send against you, in hunger and thirst, in nakedness and lack of everything. He will put an iron yoke on your neck until he has destroyed you."*
>
> (Deuteronomy 28:47-48)

Bible lesson: Before Israel is to enter the Promised Land, Moses holds assemblies with the whole nation. He reminds them of the Covenant faith that began with Abraham, and that this Covenant faith was passed down through the generations. It is theirs, and with it comes the obligation to obey God. Moses stresses that their survival as a people solely rests on their obedience to God, because God will only bless them, protect them, and make them prosperous as a people if they do His will. "If you will only obey the Lord your God, by diligently observing all His commandments that I am commanding you today, the Lord your God will set you high above all the nations of the earth; all these blessings shall come upon you and overtake you, if you obey the Lord your God" (Deuteronomy 28:1-2). Moses warns them of the curses they will incur if they are disobedient; God will withdraw his blessings and protection, and punish them. *"But if you will not obey the Lord your God by diligently* *observing all His commandments and decrees, then all these curses shall come upon you and overtake you: "The Lord will send upon you disaster, panic, and frustration in everything you attempt to do. The Lord will afflict you with consumption, fever, inflammation, with fiery heat and drought, and with blight and mildew. The Lord will cause you to be defeated before your enemies; the Lord will afflict you with madness, blindness, and confusion of mind; you shall grope about at noon as blind people grope in darkness, but you shall be unable to find your way; and you shall be continually abused and robbed, without anyone to help"* (Deuteronomy 28:15, 20, 22, 25, 28-29). **There is severe punishment for disobedience to God.**

As Israel was held in judgment by God, the faith of the PAOCC states, "I believe that human society stands under the judgment of one God..." (BCN Creed). God judges between good and evil, right and wrong. God judges our loyalty to the Covenant. The oppression, suffering, and catastrophes of our people, shown in poverty, incarceration, drug and alcohol abuse, crime against each other, sicknesses, strife and civil war, are our punishments in neglecting to do God's will. As Moses reminded Israel, the PAOCC reminds Black people today to *"diligently observe the words of this Covenant, in order that you may succeed in everything that you do."* Maintain a compatible relationship with God!

Introduction: The faith of the Pan African Orthodox Christian Church did not come full blown into being, but developed through the experiences of a people trying to maintain a compatible relationship with God. The faith of the Church teaches us that, "The Black man sought to expiate the sin of individualism for which he had been expelled from the Garden of Eden by developing a communal way of life in which each individual merged his life into the life of the group and the life of the group became more important than his own. God recognized the Black man's repentance and made His **First Covenant** with the Black patriarch, Abraham, declaring the Black Nation Israel to be His Chosen People" (BCN Statement of Faith). "I will be your God, if you will be My people." This is our struggle, to satisfy the conditions of the Covenant. We are demanded by God to obey The Law—The Ten Commandments, the revelations of the prophets, and the continuing revelations of our Holy Patriarch. The faith of the Church is not stagnant; it is always evolving as Black people struggle to do the will of God. "In this day, Black Christian Nationalism is the living prophetic voice *of God* for African people "(BCN Teaches #9).

When the Black Nation Sinned and Returned to Individualism, God Punished Them

"The Lord will scatter you among all peoples, from one end of the earth to the other, and there you shall serve other gods, which neither you nor your ancestors have known. Among those nations you shall find no ease, no resting place for the sole of your foot" (Deuteronomy 28: 64-65). These punishments came to pass each time the Black Nation Israel returned to individualism. Their sins, as stated by the prophets, were self-indulgence, injustice against the other, no fair dealing, exploitation of the poor for luxury living by the few, neglect of the needy and the orphans, worshipping other gods and adopting the materialistic, immoral rituals of idol worship. All these destroy a nation.

When God delivered Israel from Egyptian oppression, and led them into the wilderness, they, with the assistance of Aaron, built a golden calf. God punished them. "Then the Lord sent a plague on the people, because they made the calf" (Exodus 32, 35). For Solomon's sins of marrying women of other nations, and for serving their gods, God tore the kingdom from him, and gave it to Solomon's servant. Solomon's laxity to the Law directly influenced the welfare of the nation. God allowed adversaries to rise up against Solomon. Solomon's sons, Jeroboam and Rehoboam fought each other for the kingship, and because of Jeroboam's ego, he announced that he would lay on them a heavy yoke, and discipline them with scorpions. His motives were self-centered rather than what was good for the nation. The Northern Kingdom seceded because of this, and Israel became a divided nation. Jeroboam built two golden calves, and caused the people to sin. Many kings came afterwards, but only a very few obeyed God. They were a rebellious people. *"For they are faithless children, children who will not hear the instruction of the Lord"* (Isaiah 30:9). For Israel's sins, God punished them by placing them in bondage to the Edoniites, to the Babylonians where they were taken into exile, to the Chaldeans, to the Egyptians, and then to the White Greeks and Romans. It was under the domination of the Romans, that the people of Israel were dispersed and their nation destroyed.

The individualism of Black people continued, and God withdrew His blessings and protection. In Africa, Black people traded with white Arabs for selfish individualistic profit; kingdoms rose up against the other and the victor made slaves out of the defeated—the Kingdoms of Ghana, Songhay and Mali met their downfalls because of their invasion upon the other; states and tribes were concerned only with their particular people and none other; many identified with the ways of foreign people. We forgot the Covenant. In the slave trade perpetrated by the Europeans, many chiefs sold their own African slaves and tribesmen into slavery. The Black Holocaust, the horrors and brutality of the slave trade, were upon us and Black people were scattered throughout the world—The Diaspora. *Our own individualism alienated us from God and from each other.* Individualism makes it impossible for us to build a nation, and to maintain a compatible relationship with God.

In Every Generation, We Struggle to Understand and Do the Will of God

Israel tried to do the will of God and failed many times. Sometimes, they did not try hard enough, and God punished them for the nation's sins. Black men and women in every generation struggled to understand and do the will of God. They believed that the life of the group (the race) was more important than their own. Harriet Tubman freed thousands of slaves by leading them from the south to the north. When the Fugitive Slave Law of 1850 was enacted, she led them all the way to Canada, explaining that "she could not trust Uncle Sam with her people any longer" *(From Slavery to Freedom)*, Gabriel Prosser, for months, planned a revolt against slavery in Henrico County, Virginia. Gathering clubs, swords, and other weapons, he and Jack Bowler brought together over 1,000 slaves for the revolt, which was to occur on August 30, 1800, but a violent storm almost routed them. Two slaves informed the whites, and more than six hundred troops were called in. Many of the revolutionaries were arrested; thirty-five were executed. Gabriel Prosser was later executed after he refused to talk to anyone, and most of them maintained their silence. One said, "I have ventured my life in endeavoring to obtain the liberty of my countrymen, and am a willing sacrifice to their cause; and I beg, as a favor, that I may be immediately led to execution. I know that you have predetermined to shed my blood, why then all this mockery of a trial?" *(From Slavery to Freedom)*

The Civil Rights Struggle was the high point in the Black man's struggle to do the will of God. Black men and women were persecuted and discriminated against by White people through poor jobs, menial wages, poor housing, and inferior education. America intentionally suppressed Black people by laws and policies (Jim Crow Laws, the Black Code). The Black man said this was not the will of God. They organized to fight against the injustices and inequalities of second-class citizenship. The Southern Leadership Conference, The Student Nonviolent Coordinating Committee, the National Association for the Advancement of Colored People, and others worked to organize this revolution. Many Black people were mobilized and held sit-ins at segregated stores and restaurants; churches were used for rallies and meeting places to organize; freedom rides were taken by busloads of Black people; marches were held, and boycotts were staged. Freedom songs fitted the churches. Bernice Reagon, who was a student at the all-Black Albany State College and secretary of the local NAACP youth chapter, concerning the struggle said, *"What I can remember is being very alive and very clear, the clearest I've ever been in my life. I knew that every minute, I was doing what I was supposed to do. That was the way it was in jail, too, and on the marches. In 'We Shall Overcome;' there's a verse that says 'God is on our side,' and there was a theological discussion that said maybe we should say, 'We are on God's side.' God was lucky to have us in Albany doing what we were doing. I mean, what better case would He have? So it was really like God would be very, very happy to be on my side. There's a bit of arrogance about that, but that was the way it felt."* Many times, we were beaten by police, churches were bombed, Bull Connor tear gassed Black people, and fire hosed them, but Black people were trying to cast off the shackles of bondage and continued to struggle because they believed it was the will of God. God was with us and we gained a lot of victories in fair housing, better education opportunities, freedom to ride in any seat on the bus, the right to vote and access to city and government jobs.

"Therefore diligently observe the words of this Covenant in order that you may succeed in everything that you do."

The Pan African Orthodox Christian Church Calls Christians to Maintain Our Covenant Relationship with God by Giving Total Commitment to Our Struggle for Liberation

To struggle to end our oppression is the will of God. We must do whatever is necessary to carry out God's will. Black people have marched, have protested, have taken issues to court, and have gone to jail, all in the name of freedom. Today, the PAOCC, is the prophetic voice of God calling Christians to total commitment to our struggle for liberation, thus we can maintain a compatible relationship with God. We must reject individualism because this grave sin alienates us one from the other, and destroys any possibility of us building a nation. Without a powerful Black Nation, we are powerless pawns in the hands of our oppressors. We can attest to this as America reforms welfare, eliminating funds, food stamps and medical help for Black people, as affirmative action is being rescinded, as new jails are being built and Black people are used by the prison system as free labor, as insurance rates are higher than in the white suburbs, and as federal government support is taken away. The PAOCC calls Christians to accept a communal way of life; this is the only lifestyle that ensures the survival of a people, and is compatible to the will of God. The equal distribution of our tasks, affection, and spiritual energy allows us to depend on each other for our survival. Your time is needed. Your skills are needed. Your work is needed. Sacrifice and investment in Kodi, Expansion and Beulah Land (our Promised Land, 2800 acres of farmland) are needed to maintain the institutions God has given us, to expand the Church to other cities, and to be able to feed ourselves. Will you maintain a compatible relationship with God by building a nation?

So many of our people have chosen not to struggle or to only struggle a little bit, not enough to impact the work of the Church, let alone a worldwide struggle for liberation! The PAOCC is calling every Christian to maintain their Covenant relationship with God. When we obey the words of the Covenant, we will succeed as a nation in everything we do. If we choose not to obey the word of the Covenant, we shall serve our enemies. Our lives shall hang in doubt; night and day, we shall be in dread, with no assurance of our lives! Curses or blessings. Punishment or rewards. Oppression or Liberation? Man or God? Which one will you choose?

LOVE: THE GREATEST COMMANDMENT

"Revolutionary Love for Jesus, began with the Covenant and the Law....
The Covenant was GOD's guarantee that we will triumph over the forces that restrict us as a people.
The Law stated the conditions we must meet to ensure our triumph as GOD's people."

—Jaramogi

AKOMA: Love, goodwill, patience, faithfulness, fondness, endurance, and consistency
The heart.

♡ *"One of the scribes came near and heard them disputing with one another and seeing that he answered them well, he asked him, 'Which commandment is the first of all?' Jesus answered, 'The first is, Hear, 0 Israel: the Lord our God, the Lord is one; you shall love the Lord, your God, with all your heart, and with all your soul and with all your mind, and with all your strength. The second is this, 'You shall love your neighbor as yourself. There is no other commandment greater than these."*

(Mark 12: 28-31)

Bible Lesson: After Jesus' triumphal entry into Jerusalem, he entered the temple, teaching and preaching. On this occasion, one of the scribes asked Jesus which commandment was the greatest. Jesus answered him saying, "You shall love the Lord, your God. with all your heart and with all your soul, and with all your mind, and with all your strength ... You shall love your neighbor as yourself." The scribe told Jesus, *"You are right...this is much more important than all whole burnt offerings and sacrifices"* (Mark 12: 33). Then Jesus said to him, *"You are not far from the kingdom of God"* (Mark 12: 34). Jesus' mission was the revolutionary transformation of his people, which he believed could only occur through love. Jesus believed God was love. *"God, said Jesus, cares for his creatures and for mankind: He clothes the grass and feeds the ravens* (Luke 12:22); *He makes His sun* *rise on the evil and the good, and sends rain on the just and the unjust* (Matt. 5: 45); *the cheapest sparrow does not die without God's remembrance, and the very hairs of our heads are all numbered"* (Luke 12: 6-7, *Bible Dictionary*). *"God is independent, the self-existent, without beginning and end, and yet God cares!" (Bible Dictionary)* Since God is loving, and mankind is created out of the substance of God, Jesus believed that man should also love one another. Jesus revealed the meaning of love by his life. He taught forgiveness and he himself forgave many times; he felt pity for the infirm and troubled and healed them; he ate with the despised tax collectors and public sinners: he would break the Sabbath law if he could save or comfort a human life; he welcomed mothers with their children; and exhausted himself for the sake of building God's kingdom on earth and liberating his people from oppression. By his very acts, Jesus "loved his neighbor as himself." This love was a testimony that he loved God and believed that God loved him; Jesus demanded that his disciples love one another. He said, *"It is by your love that you have for one another that everyone will know that you are my disciples"* (John 12:34-35). Christians today are charged to do the same!

Individualism Is Destroying Black People

We find it difficult to love one another because we are committed to individualism; it is an evil self-destructive force, which plagues our people. Our Black condition is characterized by: Isolation, empty personal relationships, the absence of Community, powerlessness in all areas of life and poverty, which grows ever more threatening with our growing technological obsolescence (BCN Message and Mission). Our children are mis-educated and we don't possess the reading, science, math and technological skills necessary for survival in this world. We are shut out of the mainstream of America by a White power structure, which has declared us inferior, and is aggressively, dismantling our rights reaped during the Civil Rights Struggle. In light of these external forces threatening our survival, it would seem reasonable that Black people would collectively commit their time, skills, energy and income to ensure our survival, but we don't! Why? We don't love each other. Our commitment to individualism diminishes the importance of others. This makes it impossible for us to sacrifice for someone other than ourselves!

"We look at the world through individualistic eyes" (Jaramogi). Each person is trying to fight for his own self-survival, so we walk over people. We have walked over so many until we have blood up to our knees. The source of conflict in many marriages is that each spouse figures "what you can do for me," not "what we can do together." Looking at the world through individualistic eyes is the reason why men, and women are unfaithful to each other, and brag about their sexual conquests; the reason why we kill an ex-girlfriend and her children because "if I can't have her, nobody else will"; the reason why we don't totally participate in the Church because, "I will only do what I want to do"; the reason why we publicly embarrass and slander the names of others because, "I am upset"; the reason why we are unwilling to give our divine obligations because, "I need it for myself"; and the reason why we can't stand correction from anyone else because, "no one can criticize me". We teach our children to view the world through individualistic eyes. We tell them, "No one is going to look out for you. You must look out for yourself," and he does. Selling drugs to his own kind, stealing for what he wants, lying and cheating are all justifications for self-survival. We give our children messages that the group is secondary, and their desires and wants are primary. We are, in reality, destroying ourselves because of individualism. "In trying to fight for our individual survival, we usually end up in our group destruction" (Jaramogi).

"We talk about communalism, but we live individualism."
(Jaramogi)

Without Love, We Cannot Move from Individualism to Communalism

"Love your neighbor as yourself." Why is love the only avenue by which we are transformed from individualism to communalism? The answer can be found in the Bible as God revealed this to the prophets of the Black Nation Israel as well as to Jesus. "Love in the Old Testament is the basic character of the relationship between persons, a relationship with the qualities of devotion, loyalty, intimate knowledge and responsibility. It is not simply emotion but is the total quality of relationship. It is the force, which both initiates and maintains relationships, be it among persons or between God and man. From the highest pitch of sexual communion to the calmest and most detached kindness, the rightly ordered human relationship is one of mutuality in love." (*Bible Dictionary*, 164)

"The social life of man is an important–perhaps the most important–area of human relationships" (*Bible Dictionary*, 166). Only the concrete acts of love and loyalty can maintain a high quality of life in human society. The following specific relationships are designated as points of love in human life: Respect for others, *"Pleasant words are like a honeycomb, sweetness to the soul and health to the body"* (Proverbs 16:24). Loyalty of a friend for a friend (the Community), *"One who forgives an affront fosters friendship, but one who dwells on disputes will alienate a friend"* (Proverbs 17: 9); The adoration of people for a leader, *"But all Israel and Judah loved David; for it was he who marched out and came in leading them"* (1 Samuel 18:16); Love of the neighbors, *"You shall not take vengeance or bear a grudge against any of your people, but you shall love your neighbor as yourself; I am the Lord"* (Leviticus 19:18); The love of the individual and of society for the stranger, *"You shall love the stranger as yourself, for you were aliens in the land of Egypt"* (Leviticus 19:34); The Kindness shown to the poor and unfortunate, *"Those who oppress the poor insult their Maker, but those who are kind to the needy honor him"* (Proverbs 14:31).

To love requires concrete acts of kindness, forgiveness, loyalty, sacrifice, and respect. Since, we want to be treated as this, we must do these things unto others. To love is the journey we must take if we are to move from individualism to Communalism. If we are willing, a new life awaits us and our children and we can survive!

The Science of KUA Opens Our Energy Pathways So That We Can Love One Another.

KUA, in the Pan African Orthodox Christian Church, undertakes the difficult, yet possible task, of transforming Black people. You must seek change. Jaramogi says, "The pain, hopelessness and frustration of the Black condition cannot be changed unless those who SEEK change realize that they are in fact searching for a joyful existence with security, happiness and meaning within a communal framework of honest personal relationships" (BCN Message and Mission). Upon this, you aspire to shed the old individualistic life, and begin your journey to be opened so you can love others. You must take participation in the group seriously because it tears down the walls of individualism. To do this, the group goals are to be accepted over individual desires and whims. Participation in the group begins to release energy blocks where you begin to feel differently, and you become conscious of how you affect others. The group confronts behavior that disrupts and alienates members. You become aware that you don't like the feeling of being alienated or to alienate; you would rather have good relationships with others. The responsibility of treating others with love becomes a motivating force for you, and each day you realize that in helping others, a change in energy occurs. As you love your brothers and sisters as yourself, you sincerely want them to live and the only way this is ensured is through communalism.

The disciplines of the Church, meditation, Yoga, Tai Chi, devotionals and worship service are designed to open you, and keep you opened so you can function on the level pleasing to God, loving one another in a communal society. The benefits of communalism far outweigh the spoils of individualism. Happiness, security, health, and meaning cannot be purchased with money, but come only because of the quality of loving relationships. Our survival, both physically and spiritually, is totally dependent upon Love and Communalism.

There is no greater commandment than this to love God and to love your neighbor as yourself.

I BELIEVE IN JESUS CHRIST

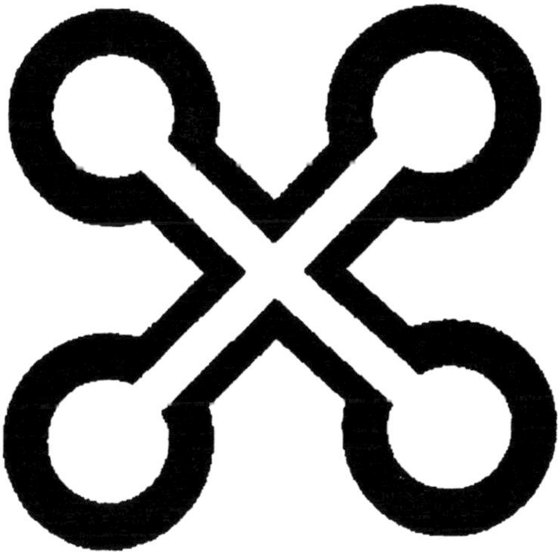

"...GOD reconciled men unto Himself in the life and teachings of Jesus, which gave them a new conception of human dignity and inspired them to fight to be men instead of slaves. GOD was in Jesus and He is in anyone who is willing to dedicate his life to the Liberation Struggle."

—Jaramogi

NYAME NWU NA MAW: Omniscience and omnipresence of GOD; the perpetual existence of man's spirit.
I live not when GOD is not.

"By this we know that we abide in him and he in us, because he has given us of his Spirit and we have seen and do testify that the Father has sent His Son as the Savior of the world. God abides in those who confess that Jesus is the Son of God, and they abide in God. So we have known and believe the love that God has for us."

(1st John 4:13-16)

Bible Lesson: The First Letter of John written to the Christian churches is a profession of faith in Jesus as the Son of God, and the Savior of the world. Some of us have questioned if Jesus is the savior of the world. The answer is "Yes." Jesus revealed the will of God as to how mankind should live, not only for Israel, but also for the whole world. The letter indicates two tests that a Christian must pass. One is that a Christian believes in the utter goodness of God. The other is that a Christian is one who believes that Jesus is the Christ (Christ means the anointed one; the Messiah); that the human Jesus is the incarnate Son of God, who perfectly reveals the will of God. "The Son of God was revealed for this purpose to destroy the works of the devil" (1st John 3:8).

Introduction: Today, we want to clear up any theological confusion about Jesus so that we might take him more seriously, and become Christians in our hearts. The Prophet

Isaiah wrote, *"For a child has been born for us, a son given to us; authority rests upon his shoulders; and he is named Wonderful Counselor, Mighty God, Everlasting Father, Prince of Peace. His authority shall grow continually, and there shall be endless peace...He will establish and uphold the kingdom with justice and with righteousness from this time onward and forevermore. The zeal of the Lord of hosts will do this"* (Isaiah 9:6-7). Isaiah prophesied around 700 B.C., the coming of the Messiah, as God's fulfillment of the First Covenant made with Abraham. The Messiah would be the righteous ruler of the Kingdom of God. He would liberate Israel and bring salvation to the world. Isaiah proclaimed that the "zeal of the Lord of hosts will do this," meaning God would intervene in the affairs of mankind. Believing in the divinity of Jesus is what makes us Christians. Without this faith, we are at best shallow and lack any real loyalty to him or to God. "Everyone who believes that Jesus is the Christ has been born of God" (1st John 5:7).

I Believe in Jesus Christ, Our Lord and Savior!

Around 200 B.C., the Essenes set themselves apart from the corruption of the world. They built communal societies and lived righteously by keeping the Covenant, obeying the Law and the teachings of the prophets. They prepared for God to intervene by sending a Messiah to save Israel from sin and oppression. This Messiah would possess Godpower, and carry out the will of God on earth. Their fervent prayers, and righteous living influenced God to act. God intervened and the whole cosmos gave birth to Jesus. The star shone on the night he was born, the angelic host proclaimed his birth, and the wise men offered gifts to the newborn King of Israel.

The Bible and our Holy Patriarch teach us that the ways of the world are evil because of the individualistic desire to serve self rather than God and others. 1st John 1: 5-16 reads, "Do not love the world or the things in the world. The love of the Father is not in those who love the world; for all that is in the world—the desire of the flesh, the desire of the eyes, the pride in riches—comes not from the Father but from the world." Jaramogi teaches that, *"The world system is an enemy system consisting of institutions from which we are excluded and which serve the interests of our oppressor. This system is built on the concept of individualism"* (Jaramogi). To accept the values, materialism, sensualism and escapism that this system offers is to sin against God.

We believe that Jesus was not a part of the world system, but of the divine system. *"There is a divine system in which we live, move, and have our being....It emanates from God who is Cosmic Energy and Creative Intelligence which created and controls the universe"* (Jaramogi). Harmony, balance, and love abound in the divine system.

"As Christians, we believe that Jesus Christ was a revelation sent by God to redeem us of our sins"(Jaramogi). Revelation means "God's manifestation of Himself to man." Redeem means to free from the bondage of sin. When we say, I believe in Jesus Christ, our Lord and Savior, we are acknowledging that we live in a sinful world, and are sinners! When we say, "I believe in Jesus Christ, our Lord and Savior", we have faith that Jesus saves us because he shows us the way to God. We believe in the divinity of Jesus, "and we have seen and do testify that the Father has sent His Son as the Savior of the world."

We Share The Faith of Jesus of Nazareth

As Christians, we must believe what Jesus believed! The Synoptic Gospels (Matthew, Mark, Luke and John) express the faith of Jesus. Jesus believed in the Power of God, and sought the experience of God as he walked the dangerous Jericho Road to Jerusalem to be baptized in the Jordan River. "He saw the Spirit of God descending like a dove and alighting on him. And a voice from heaven said, *'This is My Son, the Beloved, with whom I am well pleased"* (Matthew 3: 16-17). "Like Jesus, we too, seek the experience of God" (KUA Affirmation 2). He believed in the Covenant, the Law and the prophets. *"Do not think that I have come to abolish the law or the prophets; I have come not to abolish, but to fulfill"* (Matthew 5; 17) "Like Jesus, we accept the Covenant, the Law and the Prophets as Revelations of God, binding upon His chosen people." He believed in justice. (KUA Affirmation 1). *"The Spirit of the Lord is upon me, because He has anointed me to bring good news to the poor...to let the oppressed go free"* (Luke 4:18). "Like Jesus, we will fight the injustice, oppression, and exploitation of all Black people" (BCN Covenant). In the wilderness, he rejected the temptations of Satan and renounced the slave culture by which Satan sought to tempt him. *"Jesus said to him, 'Away with you, Satan! For it is written, Worship the Lord your God, and serve only Him'"* (Matthew 3:10). "Like Jesus, we too, renounce Satan and all his ways. We renounce the slave culture, which tempts us with materialism, sensualism, and escapism. We place God first in our lives" (KUA Affimiation 3).

When everyone follows the divine teachings of Jesus, the world will change from its state of evil and sin to the righteous Kingdom of God on earth. There will be no oppression, no selfishness, no greed of materialism, no senseless murders, no escapism, no starvation, and no poverty. When you follow the divine teachings of Jesus, your life will change, and you will be rooted in Christ, not on a superficial and perfunctory level, but on a real and solid foundation. Jesus is the redemption of all mankind. We believe there is Godpower in his name, and salvation in his teachings. *We believe in the divinity of Jesus, "and we have seen and do testify that the Father has sent His Son as the Savior of the world."*

As Members of the Pan African Orthodox Christian Church, We Embody the Revolutionary Power of God Revealed in Jesus

As Black Christian Nationalists, we believe that Jesus had Godpower. *"Then Jesus, filled with the power of the Spirit, returned to Galilee, and a report about him spread through all the surrounding country. He began to teach in their synagogues and was praised by everyone"* (Luke 4:14-15). He taught, preached and healed. *"Like, Jesus, the power of the Holy Spirit is available to us. We, too, have the power to teach, preach, and heal"* (KUA Affirmation 4). Do you believe this?

As Black Christian Nationalists, we believe that the power of God embodied in Jesus was bestowed upon his disciples at Pentecost. "After their betrayal and flight, the disciples came back together for prayer and meditation." *"All these were constantly devoting themselves to prayer together with certain women, including Mary the mother of Jesus, as well as his brothers"* (Acts1:14). When the Holy Spirit touched them at Pentecost, they were anointed the Messianic Community. *"And suddenly from heaven there came a sound like the rush of a mighty wind, and it filled the entire house where they were sitting...All of them were filled with the Holy Spirit"* (Acts 2: 2,4). Do you believe this? *"Today, we accept this Church as the Messianic Community with the Mission and the Power which Jesus had during his life-time. Everything which Jesus did, we can do"* (KUA Affirmation 7). Do you believe?

God is looking for a few good Christians who believe in His awesome Power and goodness. God is looking for a few good Christians who believe He can intervene at any time in history at His own will! God is looking for a few good Christians who do not doubt the Power of Jesus, His anointed Son, The Wonderful Counselor, The Prince of Peace, Our Lord and Savior! Will you believe today, so that we may rightfully be called the disciples of Jesus? Will you say, "I believe in the divinity of Jesus, and we have seen and do testify that the Father has sent His son as the Savior of the world."

I Believe In Jesus Christ,
Our Lord and Savior!

VISIONS OF A NEW WORLD

"We now seek to find wholeness and the maximum activation of our GOD-given human powers by rejecting an evil world and becoming part of a Transforming Community in which we can be changed. The radical change, which we seek constitutes, in fact, the recreaton of man and the creation of a new world order."

—Jaramogi

FUNTUMMIREKU DENKYEMIRREKU: The need for unity where people share the same destiny

> *"At the end of forty days they returned from spying out the land. And they came to Moses and Aaron and to all the congregation of the Israelites in the wilderness of Paran, at Kadesh; they brought back word to them and to all the congregation, and showed them the fruit of the land. And they told him, 'We came to the land to which you sent us; it flows with milk and honey, and this is its fruit. Yet the people who live in the land are strong, and the towns are fortified and very large; But Caleb quieted the people before Moses, and said, 'Let us go up once and occupy it, for we are well able to overcome it.'"*
>
> (Numbers 13:25-27, 30)

Bible Lesson: The bible is a history of the Black Nation Israel, its struggle to maintain a relationship with God and to build a nation. Through the covenant, God vowed to give them a Promised Land beginning with Abraham, and passed from generation to generation. *"Then Abram fell on his face; and God said to him, 'As for Me, this is My covenant with you: You shall be the ancestor of a multitude* of nations" (Genesis 17:34). Around 1375 B.C., the people of Israel had already left Egypt, and were now approaching the Promised Land. *"The people set out from Hazeroth, and camped in the wilderness of Paran"* (Numbers 12:16). Moses, obeying the command of the Lord, sent out twelve spies. *"Go up there into the Negeb, and see what the land is like, and whether the people who live in it are strong or weak, whether the land is* *rich or poor*" (Numbers 13:17-20). To get into the Promised Land required an awareness of reality, which is exactly what they had to face. They would have to fight other nations, protect their own, plant crops for themselves, and build their own towns and institutions. After surveying the land for forty days, the twelve spies returned. Before Moses and Aaron, and the whole congregation of Israel, they said the land is rich. It flows with milk and honey; the towns are very large and fortified, and the people are strong. Caleb said, *"Let us go up at once, occupy it, for we are well able to overcome it."* This was the attitude of one who has a vision of a new world, and who is willing to struggle and overcome the obstacles that stand in the way of getting it. But, the other ten spies said, *"We are not able to go up against this people, for they are stronger than we...and to ourselves we seemed like grasshoppers, and so we seemed to them"* (Numbers 13: 31, 33). This was the attitude of a people who wanted a Promised Land, but were too afraid and unwilling to sacrifice and struggle to take it. Their acceptance of oppression created a psychology of powerlessness weakening them, making them a groveling, pitiful, weak-kneed people, unwilling to take the risks to build a nation for themselves. The psychology of powerlessness warps the mind so profoundly that a people will attempt to destroy anything that forces them to change. This was true of Israel.

Moses told the people, *"The Lord is with us; please do not rebel against the Lord. But the whole congregation threatened to stone them"* (Numbers 14:9,10). Where do we stand? Do we have a vision of a new world?

Introduction: Jaramogi teaches, "We are Black. We are oppressed. We seek to end our oppression. The world system is an enemy system. You do realize that this world in which we live is organized. It isn't just running on automatic. We don't have anything to do with running it. You go to bed and get up in the morning, and do what you are told to do, but what you do has very little to do with running the system. Even when you have a decent job, you have such a small little niche in that job that the system can go on without you. The system is an enemy system, consisting of institutions from which we are systematically excluded and which serve the interests of our oppressors." We must face this reality if we are to have a vision of a new world controlled by righteous and communal Black people.

In Order for Black People to Maintain a Shared Vision of a Promised Land, We Must Have a Constant Awareness

of Our Reality

"Moses sent them to spy out the land... go up into the hill country, and see what the land is like" (Numbers 13:17). Because of our powerlessness, our importance, our usefulness, and our existence are determined by an enemy system. This held true from the time of chattel slavery, the Agrarian Age, through the Industrial Age, and now the Technological Age.

During the Agrarian Age (ownership of land, agriculture), the pre-capitalistic economies of Europe and America depended upon slave labor. The growth and trading of crop for eating and manufacturing (liquor, soap, oils) were done to meet the supply and demand of European peoples. Black people were forced through brutality to plant and harvest sugar in the sugar cane fields of the Caribbean Islands, and to plant and harvest the cotton, tobacco and fruit of the American South. Our usefulness strictly depended upon how much "cotton" we could pick. Our children, our religion, our culture and language, and our marriages meant nothing to slave owners. All were declared to be inferior. We were treated like animals, sold like cattle, branded like horses, and whipped so harshly the flesh was torn off of our backs. This was our reality — exclusion from the mainstream of America.

During the Industrial Age, (manufacture of products, factories), from the 1900's through the 1970's, America's capitalistic economy depended on the manufacture of thousands of products (cars, furniture, textile, machine parts, etc.) "This Industrial Revolution was an attempt to change the United States from that of an agricultural center to an industrial and manufacturing center. The increase in the labor force and the expanding economy and population provided an unlimited market for manufactured products" (*Tribute Booklet*, 1995). The Northern industrialists needed the slave labor of the south to maintain their growth. The victory of the North in the Civil War, gave the North access to the slaves. Because of changes in the South, we became displaced. The North aggressively recruited Black people. *"In the great* migration, *the initial line of communication was established by agents of northern companies, acting as intermediaries between employers and potential labor migrants. Agents were paid a fee for each worker they were able to produce. They would walk among Black workers, without turning, say in a low voice, 'Anybody want to go to Chicago, see me" (Farewell, We're Good and Gone).* Being controlled and manipulated, our usefulness only extended to how much profit the industries could reap from our labor. However, we were still exploited in wages, and in benefits. Since the same system controlled the prices of rent, clothing, and food, exorbitant prices were set for us to pay. Many who traveled north lived in the ghetto slums unable to make ends meet. This was our reality — exclusion from the mainstream of America.

The 1980's and reaching into the 21st century marks the Age of Technology. Computers have allowed for rapid dissemination of information, and at the same time have drastically reduced the need for human labor, especially Black people's. "Over half of today's Fortune 1000 corporations have set up videoconferencing rooms that link key facilities around the world. In these rooms, cameras zoom in on whoever is speaking, questions and answers are fielded, documents are shared and participants can discuss issues as if they were all in the same room (*Bold New World*)." Electronic neighborhoods offer electronic shopping, home banking, and on-line encyclopedias. But the most popular features are the electronic meeting rooms where millions of people discuss an unlimited number of topics to share ideas and interests. Black people are moving toward being obsolete. Our usefulness to white people has worn out. We have very limited knowledge of technology. With this ignorance, we are blind to the reality what the new millennium holds for us; complete disintegration of family, of religion, of the present social order, and ultimately our existence. We are still excluded from the mainstream of America. It is crucial that Black people share this reality because it is the only step that will allow us to share a vision of a new world.

The Black Church Has to Prepare Black People for the Many Difficult Challenges as We Move into the Next Millennium

"The Lord said to Moses, 'Send men to spy out the land of Canaan which I am giving to the Israelites" (Numbers 12:1). This was preparation to see what difficulties lay ahead.

The Black Church is the only institution controlled by Black people, and the only one to prophesy our destiny as we approach the 21st Century. Its responsibility is to give sight to the blind, to proclaim release to captives, to let the oppressed go free. Our dilemma must be proclaimed from the pulpit; the mis-education of Black children has sabotaged our existence to have a place in the world. In many African countries, education is not compulsory. "Denial of 'the means of competition' is perhaps the most single most consistent outcome of the education offered to poor children in the schools of our large cities, and nowhere is this pattern of denial more explicit or more absolute than in the public schools of New York City. Average expenditures per pupil in the City of New York in 1997 were some $5,500. In the highest spending suburbs of New York, funding levels rose above $11,000. The City of Detroit has had a

Black administration for close to two decades. But the city is poor and mainly Black and its school system, which is 89 percent Black, is so poorly funded that three classes have to share a single set of books in elementary school. 'It's not until the sixth grade 'the Detroit Free Press reports, 'that every student has a textbook'. At MacKenzie High School in Detroit, courses in word processing are taught without word processors. Students ask, 'When are we going to get to use computers?' But, their teacher says, the school cannot afford them" (*Savage Inequalities*, 1991). The Church must deal with these issues facing our survival on earth, and save the message of survival in heaven after death for another time. If not, we will all die and get to heaven before we planned to.

The Church must seek to change our people's psychology of powerlessness in order to change their attitudes and behaviors to be conducive to Nation building. The doubt, fear, intimidation, laziness, escapism, and identification with our oppressor, must all be changed. The unwillingness to sacrifice, to go beyond one's personal feelings and desires must be changed. The Black Church must say as Moses said, *"The land that we went through as spies is an exceedingly good land. If the Lord is pleased with us, He will bring us into this land"* (Numbers 14:7). If we are unwilling to build a Promised Land, we don't deserve God's blessings or the right to live.

The Pan African Orthodox Christian Church Has a Vision of a Pan-African World Community that can Mobilize Black People around One Communal Aim, Purpose, and Destiny—the Unification, Transformation and Empowerment of Black People

"And the Lord said to Moses, How long will this people despise me? And how long will they refuse to believe in Me, in spite of all the signs that I have done among them?" (Numbers 14: 11). As God lead Israel out of Egypt by a pillar of cloud in the day and a pillar of fire at night, God has given us signs. It is time now for our faith to be strengthened. The vision of a Promised Land has been handed down from generation to generation for the past 6,000 years starting with Abraham. It was passed from Marcus Garvey to our Holy Patriarch, Jaramogi Abebe Agyeman. This vision was of the unity of all African people across the world, the transformation of our minds, and the building of institutions to serve the interests of our people.

The unity of Black people requires an acceptance of the same theology, so God revealed Black Christian Nationalism to our Holy Patriarch, and it has been accepted by thousands of Black people here and abroad. We are charged by God to spread this news to more Black people. God revealed to our Holy Patriarch that the minds of Black people had to be transformed, and so the group process and the experience of God became the basis of our program. Jaramogi teaches that, "People change as a result of the group process. It's a constant pressure and the love of a community *committed* to *change* that transforms people. If you belong to a church and nobody criticizes you, everybody just goes his own way and you go your own way, you are not really a church." Jaramogi organized the group as basic to transformation, a movement from individualism to communalism. This is a sign from God. It's time for us to stop rebelling against the Lord.

The empowerment of Black people is now being done through the building of BCN Institutions. This too was revealed by God. Undergirding each institution is the same belief system, even though the development of each may take a slightly different course. BCN institutions are comprised of Missionary Training Institutes, Maccabee-Security Institution, Community Outreach Institution, Missionary Outreach Institution, and Mtoto House, the Children's Institution. Our time, energy, and skills must be directed to developing each one, so that each fully serves the interests of our people. God has given us signs. Now it is time for us to totally commit ourselves to the building of a Promised Land here on earth for both our salvation and our survival!

RESURRECTING THE MISSION

"Today, we accept this Church as the Messianic Community with the Mission and the Power that Jesus had during his lifetime. Everything that Jesus did, we can do."

—Jaramogi

AKOBEN: A call to action, readiness to be called to action

> *"Then the Lord said, 'How great is the outcry against Sodom and Gomorrah and how very grave their sin! I must go down and see whether they have done altogether according to the outcry that has come to Me, and if not, I will know". ' So the men turned from there, and went toward Sodom while Abraham remained standing before the Lord. Then Abraham came near and said, 'Will You indeed sweep away the righteous with the wicked?"*
>
> (Genesis 18: 20-33)

Bible Lesson: *"You shall be holy, for I the Lord your God am holy"* (Leviticus 19:2). This was a stipulation of the Covenant God made with Abraham, so God does judge what is righteous and what is wicked, what is moral and immoral. In our bible lesson, God appeared to Abraham as he sat at the entrance of his tent. Abraham also saw three men standing near Him; we find later that they are angels. These three were fed and cared for by Abraham. As they are about to leave to go to Sodom, God ponders should Abraham be told what is about to happen to Sodom. *"The Lord said, 'Shall I hide from Abraham what I am about to do...No, for I have chosen him, that he may charge his children and his household after him to keep the way of the Lord by doing* ***righteousness*** *and* ***justice****'"* (Genesis 18:17, 20). God said, *"How great is the outcry against Sodom and*

Gomorrah, and how very grave their sin" (Genesis 18: 21), Sodom and Gomorrah were the epitome of depravation, uncontrolled and unrestrained behaviors, in which every man did as he desired—INDIVIDUALISM. God told Abraham that He must go down to Sodom, and see if the outcry is warranted. Abraham, then questions God. *"Will you indeed sweep away the righteous with the wicked?"* The thought of this greatly disturbs Abraham. He argues, Lord, You can't slay the righteous with the wicked! The righteous fares better. You, Lord, the Judge of all the earth must do what is just! This concern should be on the hearts of all Christians, but sadly in today's world many do not believe God has the Power to punish in this lifetime. Maybe, after death! Abraham questions God because he must know himself how God acts in the world. Abraham asks, *"If there are fifty righteous people in Sodom, would you spare that place?" "And, the Lord said, 'If I find at Sodom fifty righteous in the city, I will forgive the whole place for their sake"* (Genesis 18:26). This shows that God has, God is, and God will make a distinction between the righteous and the wicked, and others will be forgiven because of the righteous. Abraham then asks, *"If there are ten righteous men, would you spare that place?" God said, Yes!* But, not even ten righteous men could be found in Sodom.

Introduction: *"God is Cosmic Energy and Creative Intelligence, the Unified Energy Field out of which all things were and are created. The nature of God is Unity as reflected in the interdependency of all of God's creations. In light of this, human life consists of a basic struggle between* ***individualism*** *and* ***communalism.*** *History records this struggle."*

(BCN Body of Knowledge)

The Primacy of Individualism in The World Today has Created a Rising Tide of Ideological Confusion

If God intended for His Chosen People to keep the way of the Lord by being righteous and just, and if this is the way mankind on a whole is suppose to live, then the world is in rebellion against God, and is in bondage to sin. Individualism is the "god of this world." Accepting individualism is wicked. Logically, in order for people to be just requires a belief that others are important and have God given value. Individualism does not take this into account. We must become keenly aware of how individualism corrupts and confuses our ideals and our beliefs.

Spiritual books of healing and of prophecy permeate the bookstores. These books are read by many, but confused Black people see them as being "handwritten by God." So, they apply the ideas of the book to their lives, and use them to interpret the bible. They come to believe they are "goddesses and gods"—spiritual mediums. They hold special spiritual sessions and have their own spiritual messages believing God has chosen them to do so. The bible, then, with its emphasis on communalism, righteousness, justice, liberation, and nation building becomes obscure to these self-ordained prophets. Instead, individualism in the forms of, "How can I make a profit, or how can I become elevated above all," becomes dominant. To keep this confusion out of the minds of the Israelites as they struggled to build a Nation, God gave this law. *"Do not turn to mediums or wizards; do not seek them out to be defiled by them; I am the Lord your God"* (Leviticus 19:31).

Individualism has confused and corrupted the churches. The former elected president of the National Baptist Association was the "leader" of over eight million Black people. The mission of the Church as expressed in Jesus' life, *"God anointed me to bring good news to the poor, to proclaim release to the captives, to let the oppressed go free* " (Luke 4:18-19) has been replaced by individualistic material gains. This minister, "used a check drawn on a church account to make a $1,000 down payment on a $36,000 diamond ring for his alleged mistress, and to buy a $135,000 car, and a $22,000 time share" (*Chicago-Sun*

Times, 1997), The leaders of the National Baptist Convention arrogantly refused to investigate these allocations. *"If there are ten righteous people, would you spare this place?"* Where are the righteous? The concept of sin is vague because no church points to **Individualism** as a grave sin. Many do not believe it is! Ideological confusion permeates every aspect of life, religion, education, government, and family, giving rise to unhappiness, violence, corruption, and a profound ignorance as to what is the will of God.

The Mission of the Church has Been Lost Because It has Abandoned the Struggle to Overcome Individualism

In the past, the Black church in America sought to meet the needs of Black people. In the rural South, Black people were well aware that we were oppressed and systematically excluded from the mainstream of America. We had to create a new communal life to survive. Black men, and especially Black women, learned to cooperate economically. We donated the little we had to build small churches. The church supported the sick, and benefited widows and fatherless children. We maintained the church by collecting funds, teaching bible class, supervising the children and organizing social events.

We found acceptance in the church. A sense of community existed, and we all knew each other.

Beginning in 1916, Black people began to migrate to the north as America became more industrialized. The transition from a communal rural life to an urban one had a profound debilitating effect upon Black people. The sense of community was all but lost in the alienating cities of the north. Families were torn apart as some migrated up north, while others remained in the south. The stark reality of loneliness, poverty, and White exploitation was more than people could bear. To escape this, Black people engaged in drugs, abuse of alcohol, and excessive partying. We became more fragmented and more individualistic. The Black church's message was that drugs, alcohol, and dancing were all sins. However, it did nothing to change the conditions of Black people. In fact, their preaching of individual salvation after death served to condition Black people even more to be individualistic.

During the Civil Rights Movement, the Black church provided institutional stability by allowing a place where meetings and rallies could be held. In a movement, everyone does what is necessary to reach its goals, and the church did. It also provided institutional stability to the movement in organization and spiritual energy. The church was engaged in the mission of gaining equality for all Black people. Moreover, the actions of Black people were focused for the good of all. In essence, we were communal.

Today, Jaramogi says, *"The Black church is dead.* "It does not promote communalism or liberation, but stamps with approval, individualism. As we grow more obsolete because of mis-education and lack of skills in a highly technological society, the Black church has abandoned the will of God for us to overcome individualism, thus becoming an obstacle to fulfillment and freedom. It no longer exists for our survival or our salvation, but only to "learn the word." Just learning the word probably makes for "do nothing Christians" who flock into the mega churches. One of these preachers said, "It is by your words, you will be justified, not your actions." This is ideological confusion because Jesus said it is what you do that makes you a disciple. The mission of the Christian is more than just learning the word. It is transforming the state of being of our people so we can change our oppressive conditions! To do this, we must act! The quest to return to our original state of being (open to the power and energy of God) pits men in a struggle to overcome their individualism as they seek to obey God by building a Communal Society or the Kingdom of God on earth" (Jaramogi).

Recognizing Communalism as a Basic Foundation to Christian Life, the Pan African Orthodox Christian Church, Calls Black People into Our Sacred Circle where God is the Cosmic Reality

The Black church can live again if it accepts its mission to restore men and women to a state of communalism. This is the only way we can be fulfilled and be inspired to struggle against our oppression. The root of the problem must be dealt with, and then the symptoms of alienation, unhappiness, corruption, violence, and immorality can change. The root is individualism, the evil and destructive value adopted by so many. To transform this state of being, we must experience God, the Power that created all of life. This transformation is done on an energy level, where our motives, beliefs, and values are changed. KUA is the process of transformation. The first step is socialization—the movement from individualism to communalism through constant pressure and love of the group to which we are assigned. This constant pressure moves us to choose the goals and concerns of the group over individualistic desires. We must be socialized first. KUA, the Science by which men and women seek to return to the state of being which God gave them at the time of creation—a state of openness, harmony, peace, and love is available for every seeker.

The PAOCC calls you to a life of communalism in which we share our resources, money, skills, and energy to build and maintain institutions so necessary for our survival. Only through the practice of communalism can we learn to love again. The Church calls us into the Sacred Circle where the Power of God is available, and demands a way of life, which will maintain our Covenant relationship with God. Our relationship with God and our communal relationships with our brothers and sisters will make us a righteous people whom God favors. Being on God's side will ensure us power, blessings, and resolutions to aid us in our struggle to free ourselves from oppression. The PAOCC is the last vestige of hope for Black people as well as mankind! Will you carry out the mission? Will you be counted as one of the righteous?

> *"For the Lord watches over the way of the righteous, but the way of the wicked will perish."*
>
> (Psalm 1:6)

WHAT DO YOU STAND FOR?

"We will make BCN the cornerstone of the Black man's sturggle for power and survival. We will build a Black communal society, which can protect the mind and bodies of Black men, women, and children everywhere."

- Jaramogi

PEMPANSIE: The need for ever-readiness, steadfastness, hardiness, valor, and fearlessness.

> *"You must therefore be careful to do as the Lord your God has commanded you; you shall not turn to the right or to the left. You must follow exactly the path that the Lord your God has commanded you, so that you may live, and that it may go well with you, and that you may live long in the land that you are to possess."*
>
> (Deuteronomy 5: 32-33)

Bible Lesson: In this time in the history of the Black Nation Israel, they are about to enter the Promised Land. Moses calls the whole assembly of Israel together to speak to them on the Law, the statutes and ordinances they must follow if they are to become a nation with God as their King. A nation is a body of people existing independently; it must share a common allegiance and a common faith, which we define as a system of beliefs. The books of Exodus, Leviticus, Numbers and Deuteronomy comprise the Law, the statutes and ordinances necessary to maintain Israel's nationhood.

Moses speaks to them about the Law, the Ten Commandments, a system of behaviors, which makes their faith in God and the Covenant real. We focus on the first Commandment of the Law and its importance. *"I am the Lord your God, who brought you out of the land of Egypt, out of the house of slavery; you shall have no other gods before Me"* (Deuteronomy 5:6-7). Why is this so important? Believing in one God, the God of the Covenant, to whom loyalty and submission are given, unifies a people into a nation because they share the same faith. When a people serve other gods, their faith and behaviors are not in accordance with the Law, the statutes and ordinances; they are a divided people. Today, many of our people have placed other gods before God. They have forgotten that God is the God of a people. Each one is trying to build some security for himself giving little regard to building security for our people.

Israel is warned of the consequences of rejecting God. *"You shall not make for yourself an idol; for I the Lord your God am a jealous God, punishing children for the iniquity of parents, to the third and fourth generation of those who reject Me"* (Deuteronomy 5:8-9). Are our children being punished because of our sins? Why are they on drugs, incarcerated, and violent? Why are some of our birth children not loyal to God? Then, Israel is reassured of God's promises if they obey. *"But I show steadfast love to the thousandth generation of those who love Me and keep My commandments"* (Deuteronomy 5:10). Israel could prosper through God's blessings and protection for a thousand generations if they love God and keep His commandments. God's Covenant promises to Israel are ours today if we love Him and practice the faith of Black Christian Nationalism! "You must therefore be careful to do as the Lord your God has commanded you."

Introduction: "I give you a mustard seed with which you can move mountains, if you have a mind to" (Jaramogi). The mustard seed is very small, but locked into this small seed are many miracles. When the seed develops and grows into a sizable plant, it provides shade for birds. It provides fodder for cattle and sheep. Even its seeds are grounded into a condiment (mustard) and used for human consumption as well as a counter irritant in plastics. The mustard seed symbolizes potential and power. Our Holy Patriarch has given us the key to unlock our potential and open us to power through the faith of Black Christian Nationalism, its teachings and processes. "Our Church is designed to open us for the experience of God. Our groups exist to mediate spiritual power. Therefore, we are able to bring all things into conformity with His will. Kugasana" (Jaramogi). Today, we ask ourselves, "What do we stand for?" Do we take this mustard seed (BCN), and become powerful or do we let the key of life slip through our fingers?"

Black Christian Nationalism is the Revealed Truth of God and the Gospel of Salvation to the World

"And what other great nation has statutes and ordinances as just as this entire law that I am

setting before you today." (Deuteronomy 4:8) After careful re-examination of the Bible, God's revealed truth is known, and the Bible and Christianity are relevant to the Black man's struggle for liberation. What is known is that God shared a covenant relationship with the Black Nation Israel. God told Abraham, *"I will make of you a great nation, and I will bless you"* (Genesis 12:2). *"I will establish My covenant between me and you, and your offspring after you throughout their generations. And I will walk among you, and will be your God, and you shall be My people"* (Genesis 17:7; Leviticus 26:12). What is known is that God is the God of a people. What is known is that Jesus was a Black Messiah sent by God to liberate Israel from Roman oppression. The coming of the Messiah was foretold in the Old Testament and his birth and anointment recorded in the New Testament. *"Now the birth of Jesus the Messiah took place in this way. And when Jesus had been baptized, the heavens were opened and the Spirit of God descended like a dove and alighted on him...The Spirit of the Lord is upon me for He has sent me to set the oppressed free"* (Matthew 1:18; 3:16-17; Luke 4:18), What is known is that Godpower was bestowed upon Jesus' disciples at Pentecost, and they carried on the revolutionary mission of Jesus. *"On the day of Pentecost, they were all together in one place...all of them were filled with the Holy Spirit...Awe came upon everyone, because many wonders and signs were being done by the apostles"* (Acts2:2,3,43). What is known is that communalism was incorporated in the First Christian Church, (revolutionary movement) and is God's purpose for all of mankind. *"All who believed were together and had all things in common"* (Acts 2:44).

Black Christian Nationalism embodies these truths of the Bible, and they are expressed in the written faith (system of beliefs inherent in the Law, statutes and ordinances) of our Church found in the BCN Covenant, the BCN Creed, BCN Teaches-Program-Philosophy, BCN Statement of Faith, BCN-Black Church as Change Agent, BCN Code (Law), and The Holy Sacraments. To be a Black Christian Nationalist means that you accept and live by the written faith of the Church, and submit to doing God's will as defined by the Church. In doing so, we build a Nation, holy and righteous to God our King, and by our example, the whole world will know the will of God. BCN is the Answer! "You must follow exactly the path that the Lord your God has commanded you, so that you may live, and that it may go well with you."

As Covenant Christians, The Bible is Our Rule of Faith

"You must observe them (statues and ordinances) diligently, for this will show your wisdom and discernment to the peoples, who, when they hear all these statutes, will say, 'Surely this great nation is a wise and discerning people!" (Deuteronomy 4:6) Black Christian Nation-alists are Covenant Christians. We share the belief that as a church community we have a special Covenant relationship with God. Each member's acts either maintain or diminish this relationship. Each member's acts either build a nation or inhibits its growth. God's demands for us are expressed in the Bible, and in the faith of Black Christian Nationalism. "Thou shall have no other gods before Me" is one demand. Living communally is another. Yet, today, too many of our members do not live by these any longer. Is it because we do not intellectually understand our faith? Or is it that we do understand, but reject parts that are uncomfortable and too demanding? Paul preached individual salvation, which we reject. However, in today's world, Paul comes in many forms. We are attracted to those who we believe have spiritual insight. Even though their writings may be interesting, they do not emphasize that salvation is a group experience, but that you

as an individual can become spiritual if you follow their advice. Who is your god? What is your rule of faith? Our commitment to individualism attracts us to those who write about individual spiritual attainment, which in turn, reinforces our own individualism, making a complete circle of sin. A lot of literature has been read and examined. Some have been found useful, and applied in the framework of Black Christian Nationalism with the intent that they will enhance group experiences. Without a BCN application, we end up confused with only a minimal commitment to a group. We may find ourselves serving other gods.

Covenant Christians believe in communalism where there is an equitable distribution of tasks, affection, and spiritual energy. To live communally requires daily decisions on behalf of the welfare and goals of the group rather than on self. This struggle against individualism is an earthly battle, and we need a group to help us fight, or we become complacent. In Deuteronomy 4:25-27, it says, "When you have had children and children's children, and become complacent in the land, thus doing evil in the sight of the Lord your God, you will soon utterly perish.... but because the Lord your God is a merciful God, He will neither abandon or destroy you; He will not forget the Covenant." *On our part, we must be careful to do as the Lord has commanded us!*

Your Belief in Black Christian Nationalism is the Only Hope For Our Survival and Salvation

"When your children ask you in time to come, 'What is the meaning of the decrees and the statutes and the ordinances that the Lord our God has commanded to you?' Then you shall say to your children, God brought us out of the darkness into the light and gave us BCN so that we can come upon Spiritual Power to liberate us from oppression and the sin of individualism. *"Then the Lord commanded us to observe all these statutes, to fear the Lord our God, for our lasting good, so as to keep us alive, as is now the case. If we diligently observe this entire commandment before the Lord our God, as He has commanded us, we will be in the right."* (Deuteronomy 6:20, 24-25)

Is BCN still your faith? Is it what you stand for? Are you still in the right? When we look at the world, we can see all the trouble the world is in. Civil war and massacres in the Congo, starvation in the Sudan, government policies denying funds for school clinics, consciously murdering another for disability or accident insurance, all these indicate that the sin of individualism is the root of corruption and destruction. BCN is the Answer because it teaches that communalism can bring peace, stability, and meet the needs of all. Communalism acknowledges that each person has God given value, intrinsic at his/her birth. With this most important perception of others, it would be difficult to mistreat or exploit another human being.

Is BCN still your faith? Is it what you stand for? Are you still in the right? When we look at the disasters of hurricanes, floods, global warming, heat waves, pollution, and all manner of diseases, we can see that the world is in trouble. We need Godpower to intervene and to help deliver us. BCN is the Answer because it provides the environment and processes that open our groups to spiritual power. We have been blessed to live in a safe environment, free of crime, drugs, and violence. We are blessed to have devotionals, one of the most powerful processes, which opens us to spiritual power. We need spiritual power so that we may be healed and transformed; then we can mediate it and change the world. "I give you a mustard seed by which you can move mountains if you have the mind to..." Jaramogi's message is the same message Moses gave his people, as they were about to enter the Promised Land.

God is calling each one of us to be Black Christian Nationalists, to deepen our faith, to increase our works, to build a Nation, and to stand for Him. Will you answer, Yes! Will you make BCN your Choice?

Some folks would rather have houses and land.
Some folks choose silver and gold,
But these things that they treasure
And forget about their souls,
We've decided BCN is our Choice!

Some folks would rather be slaves all their lives.
Some folks choose integration
But these things that they treasure
And forget about their souls,
We've decided BCN is our Choice!

The road is rough, and the going gets tough.
And the hills are hard to climb
We started out a long time ago,
There is no doubt in our minds,
We've decided BCN is our Choice!

WE ARE BUILDING A TEMPLE FOR GOD

"The Kingdom of God has come!
We are in the Kingdom.
The Kingdom is within us
And we wait patiently for its coming."

—Jaramogi

NYAME DUA: God's presence and protection.
An altar of God.

"Solomon sent word to King Huram of Tyre: 'Once you dealt with my father David and sent him cedar to build himself a house to live in. I am now about to build a house for the name of the Lord my God and dedicate it to Him for offering fragrant incense before Him, and for the regular offering of the rows of bread, and for burnt offerings morning and evening, on the Sabbaths and the new moons and the appointed festivals of the Lord our God, as ordained forever for Israel. The house that I am about to build will be great, for our God is greater than other gods."

(2 Chronicles 2:3-5)

Bible Lesson: It is amazing to speak on the wisdom of King Solomon, on him being raised not only in royalty, but in the Covenant faith of Israel by his father King David, on his diplomacy and success as a merchant elevating Israel to a position of power and prosperity through trade; on his leadership skills as he organized the Kingdom of Israel into twelve districts with a prefect over each to bring them under his jurisdiction, and on his intelligence to hold together a nation which was now also inhabited by over 150,000 conquered peoples. But, to see his love for God in all that he did is even more amazing. Solomon sought an experience with God. *"Solomon went up there to the bronze altar before the Lord, which was at the tent of meeting and offered a thousand burnt offerings on it. That night God appeared to Solomon, and* *said to him, 'Ask what I should give you'"* (2 Chronicles 1:7). King Solomon asked God to fulfill the promise made to his father David, to grant him wisdom and knowledge to rule over Israel, who was now as numerous as the dust of the earth. God answered Solomon, saying you did not ask for wealth, possessions, honor, or not even a long life, but you asked for wisdom and knowledge. This I grant you, and I will also give you riches and honor.

In the four hundred and eightieth year after the people of Israel came out of Egypt, the fourth year of the reign of King Solomon, he wrote a letter to the King of Tyre, and said I am about to build a house for the name of my God. I am going to do it even though I ask myself, *"Who am I to build a house for Him, since heaven, even highest heaven cannot contain Him"* (2 Chronicles 2:6). I want you to send me an artisan skilled to work in gold, silver, bronze, and iron, and in purple, crimson, and blue fabrics, trained also in engraving to join the skilled workers who are with me. Send me also cedar, cypress, and algum timber from Lebanon. I will provide for your servants (2 Chronicles 2:7-10). Solomon mobilized an entire nation to build the temple of God. He assigned his own skilled workers and ordered the 150,000 aliens in the land to be the laborers. *"In the most holy place he made two carved cherubim and overlaid them with gold. He adorned the house with settings of precious stones. He lined the house with gold—its beams, its thresholds, its walls, and its doors; and he carved cherubim on the walls"* (2 Chronicles 3:3-15). When the temple was finished, the whole congregation assembled to witness the dedication and the Ark of the Covenant being brought to the House of God. The Levites blew their trumpets, and played in unison with the singers as they praised and gave thanksgiving to God. Solomon prayed to God, *"Now rise up, 0 Lord God, and go to Your resting place, You and the ark of Your might, When Solomon ended his prayer, fire came down and consumed the burnt offering; and the glory of the Lord filled the temple."*

The temple, in all its magnificence, symbolized the presence of God and the responsibility of Israel to live by God's will. It was King Solomon's message that Israel was to commit their lives to God, and that God would keep His Covenant promises. We, too, are called to commitment!

The Mission of the Church Must Grow Out of Our Basic Christian Commitment to Live in Complete Service to God

In 1953, God called into being the Pan African Orthodox Christian Church for the liberation and survival of Black people, as well as to establish His kingdom on earth. Our founders committed their lives to this mission, to build the Temple for God—A Righteous Black Nation with power. Based on the revelations of God's will in the Old Testament, and the teachings of Jesus, the Black Messiah, in the New Testament, our founders' position was "The officers and members of the Shrines of the Black Madonna believe that the Black Church can become relevant to the Black Revolution. Upon the foundation of this faith we have undertaken to build a 'Black Nation within a Nation', following the teachings of the Black Messiah, Jesus of Nazareth" (BCN Manifesto). Jesus labored in love to heal, to teach, and to deliver his people from oppression. He taught them to seek an experience with God, and a communal relationship with their fellow brothers and sisters, and to commit themselves to building the Kingdom of God on earth.

Our founders labored in love and worked to make the mission of the church more effective. They launched a fight against the Detroit school system, they organized the Inner City Organizing Committee to fight against injustice, formed the Citywide Citizens Action Committee, a federation of several Black organizations to deal with economic development projects, they published the Illustrated News, a newspaper confronting issues in the Black community, and, they gave sacrificially to purchase property for the building of our institutions, Shrine 1, 2, 3, Cultural Center 1, and Beulah Land. They began to develop the process by which "individuals" could be transformed by life in the Black Nation. They envisioned a Mtoto House (Children's Community), and expansion Shrines all over the world. It was the commitment of our founders who laid the foundation for the Temple of God. They said, "We understand God in terms of the Liberation Struggle. We interpret Jesus in terms of the Liberation Struggle. We define the role of the Church in terms of the Liberation Struggle. We seek Christian Commitment in terms of the Liberation Struggle" (BCN Manifesto).

As Members of The Church, Our Commitment is Based Upon Our Acceptance of Responsibility for Others

"Give your servant therefore an understanding mind to govern your people, able to discern between good and evil; for who can govern this Your great people?" King Solomon's commitment was based upon his acceptance of responsibility for his people, Israel. His prayer was to govern them with an understanding mind. Our founders' commitment was also based upon their acceptance of responsibility for Black people. In the BCN Manifesto, it states, "We must restructure our relationships within the Black Nation in

terms of unity and love in preparation for a realistic power struggle against oppression. Members accepted the same responsibility as our founders, to learn to love, to unify, and to belong to Black people. Acceptance of the BCN Covenant, which states, "To this sacred brotherhood, I commit my life", was basic. The responsibility of carrying out the Church's original mission was our purpose for living.

Something happened! The Church's original mission has been supplanted by our own individual missions. We all must examine our lives, and ask, "What is my mission?" To become a professional in some area, (an artist, or a sports athlete), I consider an achievement. Even though achievement is an innate drive, what purpose do we serve? Most of our achievements have been defined by a capitalistic system. Maybe this is why we still feel empty inside. A lot of us are going to college looking for social acceptability. We are dedicated to school, but do not know what we are doing! Going to college certainly hasn't deepened our Christian lives. Some of us feel that the Church does not understand what we are trying to do, but the truth is we do not understand what the Church is trying to do! We have become 'Sunday Only Christians.' Some of us have part-time jobs, and still participate part-time! In our self-absorbed state, we take very little responsibility for others. The building of God's temple has almost come to a standstill. If we are to carry out the original mission, we must recommit ourselves, and be responsible for saving the lives of those whom we struggle with by doing whatever the Church has deemed necessary for our survival! This is the only way we can deliver our people from oppression!

The Pan African Orthodox Christian Church Calls All Black People to Commit Themselves to a Revolutionary Religious Movement Dedicated to the Transformation and Empowerment of Our People Everywhere

"The house that I am about to build will be great, for our God is greater than other gods." The Church calls you to recommitment on this Anniversary occasion to do the things that the Nation needs! We need commitment on all levels. Maintenance workers are needed to maintain the institutions and the land God has given us. House parents are needed with the commitment to raise a Nation child as their own training him/her to become responsible, motivated, and committed to building God's temple. Cooks are needed for the nourishment and feeding of God's people. Group leaders are needed to assist in the transformation of those assigned to his care by facilitating each member's movement from individualism to communalism. Maccabees are needed to protect our

property and our lives. Missionary Outreachers are needed to economically maintain our Nation, and for expansion in the near future. Workers and those trained in agriculture are needed to make Beulah Land functional. The Church calls you today to do what the Nation needs!

Will you help build God's temple by accepting our founders original mission? Jaramogi, the founder and Holy Patriarch, Dr. Albert B. Cleage, Sr. and Mrs. Pearl Cleage, Cardinal Nandi, Bro. Oscar Hands, Hugh and Henry Cleage, Alice Strauther, Mrs. Ida Washington, Mrs. Cleo McCoy, Mrs. Lucille Watkins and the rest of our cherished charter members laid the foundation in solid gold to God's temple! What they built is only maintained by us. So, each Anniversary Month we recommit our lives. The temple we are building is God's Kingdom—A Righteous Black Nation with power for both our salvation and our survival. Will you contribute straw or cedar to the Temple of God? Will you contribute shifting sand or gold to the Temple of God? Will you be the skilled and committed worker? Recommit your lives now for the Temple we are building is great because our God is greater than other gods.

THE VISION OF A PROMISED LAND

"We labor in Love and Communal Fellowship to build a promised land. We are destined to inherit the Earth."

—Jaramogi

BESE SAKA: Affluence, power, abundance, plenty, togetherness, and unity.

> *"As Pharaoh drew near, the Israelites looked back, and there were the Egyptians advancing on them. In great fear the Israelites cried out to the Lord. They said to Moses, 'Was it because there were no graves in Egypt that you have taken us away to die in the wilderness? Is this not the very thing we told you in Egypt? Let us alone and let us serve the Egyptians? For it would have been better for us to serve the Egyptians than to die in the wilderness. But Moses said to the people. 'Do not be afraid, stand firm, and see the deliverance that the Lord will accomplish for you today; for the Egyptians whom you see today you shall never see again. The Lord will fight for you, and you have only to keep still.'"*
>
> (Exodus 14:10-14)

Bible Lesson: God's intent for Israel to become a great nation and to build a Promised Land was accepted by the First Patriarch, Abraham, and also by Moses. Most Black preachers will not tell their congregations that it is God's will for Black people to build a nation for their own race because they look at the world through White eyes. The White oppressor doesn't want us to build a nation because it threatens his power structure, and blind Black preachers feel the same because they identify with the oppressor. But, God's will is emphatically stated, "I will make of you a great nation." The struggle to become a nation to fulfill the vision of a Promised

Land continued when the Israelites were enslaved in Egypt. God chose Moses to go to Pharaoh and tell him to, "let My people go." God, in all power, sent ten plagues upon Egypt to force them to let Israel go, and the Egyptians did. As Moses organized to move over two million people from an oppressive condition, he was faced with the difficult challenge to consistently motivate them to take the risk of depending on themselves for survival. They had grown weak and afraid because of their oppression. *"God did not lead them by way of the land of the Philistines; For God thought. 'If the people face war, they may change their minds and return to Egypt. So God led the people by the roundabout way of the wilderness toward the Red Sea"* (Exodus 13:17-18). God told Moses, "I will harden Pharaoh's heart so that he might pursue you...I will gain glory for myself over Pharaoh and all his army; and the Egyptians shall know that I am the Lord." With over 600 chariots and officers, Pharaoh and his army advanced on the Israelites. When the Israelites looked back and saw them, they were afraid. They cried and wailed to Moses, "Let us alone and let us serve the Egyptians." This is the typical response of a people who accept their oppression. They feel helpless and think their only hope is in changing the conscience of the oppressor to accept them. "Let us alone and let us serve the Egyptians.' Moses told them, "Do not be afraid, stand firm, and see the deliverance that the Lord will accomplish today.' The Bible teaches us that God works on the behalf of Black people as they struggle to build a Promised Land on earth.

Introduction: *The Promised Land is a group of people living together and sharing a communal way of life with love for each other within a powerful and righteous nation"* (Jaramogi). This is evidenced in the Bible when God told Abraham to separate himself from the people of Chaldea, and establish a nation, a Promised Land on earth. "This theme of separatism as opposed to integration is a recurring theme in the Old Testament" (Jaramogi). God said, "I will be your God and you will be My people...and I will give to you, and to your offspring after you, all the land of Canaan, for a perpetual holding." If we want God to act for us against oppression and injustice, then we must maintain the vision of a Promised Land. It was difficult for the Black Nation Israel, and it is equally difficult for Black people today because we identify with our oppressor rather than God's will for us to struggle to build a Promised Land. Without this vision and purpose in life, we are like ghostly dark shadows whose time is running out because of the setting sun; and when it sets, the shadows are lost in a world of darkness, no form, no substance, no survival.

The Bible Reveals to Us The Religious Struggle of a People Who Faced the Difficult Challenges of Maintaining the Shared Vision of a Promised Land on Earth

The shared vision of a Promised Land began with God's covenant with Abraham and was passed down from generation to generation as a sign of God's will. The shared vision depended upon Israel's identification with God and with their people. *"Then God spoke all these words: I am the Lord your God, who brought you out of the land of Egypt, out of the house of slavery, you shall have no others gods before Me"* (Exodus 20:1-2). *"You shall not take vengeance or bear a grudge against any of your people, but you shall love your neighbor as yourself, I am the Lord"* (Leviticus 19:18). *"For you are a people holy to the Lord your God; the Lord your God has chosen you out of all the peoples on earth to be His people, His treasured possession"* (Deuteronomy 7:6). The entire history of Israel relates to their religious belief that God intended for them to live as a free people in a Promised Land.

In the wilderness, Moses by the guidance of the Holy Spirit sought to socialize the Israelites to become the people of God. They were a stubborn people weakened by a slave mentality. *"The whole congregation complained against Moses and Aaron in the wilderness. They said to them, 'if only we had died by the hand of the Lord in the land of*

Egypt, when we sat by the fleshpots and ate our fill of bread; for you have brought us out into this wilderness to kill this whole assembly with hunger'" (Exodus 16:1-4). Moses instituted the Law of God and the transformative practices of rituals and observances to change the values and belief system of the Israelites. The vision of a Promised Land continued as Moses undertook the task of trying to transform his people.

In the Conquest of the Promised Land, Israel had to fight in war against powerful African nations. Joshua, the commander of the army, strategized, and fought the battle of Jericho, driven by the vision of a Promised Land. *"The Lord said to Joshua, 'This day I will begin to exalt you in the sight of all Israel, so that they may know that I will be with you as I was with Moses...Joshua said to the people, 'Shout! For the Lord has given you the city'"* (Joshua 63:7:6:16). The vision of a Promised Land continued through warfare.

In the Period of the Judges, when there was no king in Israel, holy men and women were called by God to bring some governmental structure and social control in an attempt to hold Israel together because the Promised Land also depended on the state of mind and the quality of relationships among the people. *"Then the Lord raised up judges, who delivered them out of the power of those who plundered them. Yet, they did not listen to their judges"* (Judges 2:16-19).

In each generation, the vision of Abraham was kept alive through the struggles of men and women who also answered God's call, even through the time of Jesus. But, these were few compared to the masses of Israelites who refused to struggle for a Promised Land.

A People Who Lack a Shared Vision Find it Difficult, If Not Impossible, To Sustain the Tedious, But Necessary Tasks Involved in Nation Building. Consequently, They Succumb to the Same Negative Forces Designed to Keep Them Oppressed and Fragmented

Jaramogi teaches us that we find it difficult to share a vision of a Promised Land because *"Black people are not fully convinced that we have an enemy."* Even though we were snatched from our Motherland Africa and packed on slave ships unfit for human survival, we are not fully convinced that we have an enemy. Even though one hundred million died in the Middle Passage across the Atlantic Ocean, we are not fully convinced that we have an enemy. Even though, we were lynched, hung with bodies riddled with bullets, tarred and feathered, and castrated, we are not fully convinced that we have an enemy. Even though two white policeman committed acts of racism by sodomizing a Black man, even though affirmative action has been declared unconstitutional, even though new radical white mayors are privatizing their cities shutting out Black people, even though Africa is still being raped of its resources by Europeans, even though our children are mis-educated and less money is spent on them than on White students, even though new district lines have been re-drawn to decrease our voting power, even though America is moving to White conservatism and acts of racism are more overt, and even though inner cities are abandoned and look like ghost towns, we are still not fully convinced we have an enemy.

We are exploited and oppressed by an evil world system, set up and controlled by White people who sit on seats of politics, education, and corporations who make decisions that affect our future and the lives of our children. This is why life is so bad! Black people's response to oppression is to rationalize our conditions by explaining how far we have come in obtaining jobs, education and money. Even though for a few of us this is so, too many still live in poverty, are unemployed, unskilled, and are homeless; therefore, collectively whether lower or middle class, we are still powerless. Why? An evil world system works against the best interests of Black people. Yet, we are confused about this reality because we go to school with White people, work with them and date them. We think it is a colorblind society, which is only a camouflage for the far-reaching forces at work that determine our education, where we live, or whether we get government assistance.

The tentacles of the evil world system touches every aspect of our lives, determining prices on all consumer products, raising taxes, raising or lowering interest rates, controlling television programs, deciding on minimal wages, and many others. However, in the midst of an enemy system, we are almost relegated to accepting what little we can get from it, rather than struggle for a nation of our own. We exhibit the same behaviors that keep us oppressed—the individual concern, quest for material possessions, apathy towards Church functions and obligations, and irresponsibility towards the welfare of all Black people. Thus, we identify more with the oppressor's world. Until we are able to understand the existence and complex operations of this system, the tasks involved in building a better world for ourselves escape us. Jaramogi says, "To identify with the oppressor is to accept his myth of our own inferiority." In this state, we work harder to build his world than to build our own.

"Emotional involvement is not enough to keep you committed to the struggle"

—Black Christian Nationalism

The Pan African Orthodox Christian Church Calls All Black People to Dedicate Their Lives to The Shared Vision of a New Promised Land on Earth. Through a Pan-

African World Community, Grounded in Communalism, God's Power Can Come to Bear to Change Our Earthly Conditions.

"The Black church has the task of trying to lead Black people to a Promised Land of which many cannot even conceive. This is the first step. Black people must be able to dream of living together with love and dignity, and desire this kind of world for themselves and their children. If we can accept the possibility and desirability of this kind of Black communal living, then we can begin to program for its realization. We have only to determine realistically what we must do to build here on earth the dream which already exists in our minds" (Black Christian Nationalism). This takes an intellectual understanding of the struggle. The enemy must be defined as the enemy of our people. With this realization, we are willing to go through the training that prepares us to build our Promised Land. "You must participate in a training program involving lectures, discussions, and readings. You must come to understand the position of the church and the nature of the Liberation Struggle. You must learn a point of view, a philosophy, and a theology before you can participate meaningfully in the life of the church" (Black Christian Nationalism).

With training, the institutions of the PAOCC become more meaningful, and we see them for what they are... the institutions of our Black nation. The Maccabees—Our Security Institution. Mtoto House Our Children's Institution. Missionary Training Institutes—Our Training Institutions. Community Outreach—Our Recruitment Institution. Kuumba Kitchen—Our Dining Institution. KUA—Our Transforming Institution. Missionary Outreach—Our Fund Raising Institution. With a shared vision, we struggle hard each day to develop our institutions to a highly efficient level. We do not ever give up for these are ours; our keys to unlock the gates of the Promised Land.

"Do not be afraid, stand firm and see the deliverance that the Lord will accomplish for you today." It is God's will that we build our Promised Land. Jaramogi, says we must start with the church; it is the only institution that we control. No matter how bad churches are today, if only they take on new directions to lead the struggle to build a Promised Land, then God will surely deliver us. If we seek God daily, through the group process, and the spiritual disciplines of the church, we become open to receive Godpower and have more energy and intelligence to carry out our struggle to the day we die. *"Stand firm, and see the deliverance that the Lord will accomplish for you today."* Our nation will rise again! Share the vision of the Promised Land.

BEULAH LAND: GOD'S PROMISED LAND

"I will bring you into the land I swore to give to Abraham, Isaac and Jacob; I will give it to you for a possession. I am the Lord."

—Isaiah 6:8

NYAME NTI: By GOD's Grace.
Faith and Trust in GOD.
Since GOD exists, I will not feed on leaves...."

> *"You shall be a crown of beauty in the hand of the Lord and a royal diadem in the hand of your God. You shall no more be termed Forsaken, and your land shall no more be termed Desolate; but you shall be called My Delight Is in Her, and your land shall be called, Beulah, for the Lord delights in you."*
> (Isaiah 62: 3-4)

Bible Lesson: *"Hear, O heavens, and listen O earth; for the Lord has spoken: I reared children and brought them up, but they have rebelled against Me"* (Isaiah 1: 2). Such were the conditions of the Black Nation Israel. They had violated their Covenant relationship with God through self-serving, individualistic behaviors. *"Ah, sinful nation, people laden with iniquity, offspring who do evil, children who deal corruptly, who have forsaken the Lord, who have despised the Holy One of Israel"* (Isaiah 1:4). This caused the energy level of the nation to be at an all time low. Israel was dying because they had cut themselves off from the power-energy of God and at the same time was threatened by the powerful Assyrians. It was to these conditions, Isaiah was called by God to prophesy and to lead Israel back to God. When God asked, *"Whom shall I send, and who will go for us?" Isaiah said, 'Here am I, send me'"* (Isaiah 6, 8).

Introduction: "For I the Lord love justice" (Isaiah 61: 8). In today's world, Western

Civilization is deteriorating because it embraces individualism; this is evident in the injustices of this society. The government no longer protects the poor, but abuses them even more by taking away the safety nets of welfare, Medicaid, and affirmative action. The federal government now gives each state block grants to take care of the poor, but the states prefer to spend the funds on other matters and seek to get rid of welfare. The workforce in which companies are to hire all of those eliminated from welfare rolls, will not work because they can not absorb millions of displaced people. As a result, our conditions are getting worse, more homelessness, more starvation, more joblessness, more college dropouts, and more desperation. Black people will migrate from state to state hoping for some kind of aid, but they will not find any! We envision the next ten years to be crises years for Black people. We must figure out what to do! Our answer: Beulah Land must become our major undertaking to meet the crises!

Isaiah believed in the Covenant and in the Promised Land. His faith and his actions constituted an energy involvement in what God called him to do. He spoke against Israel's alliance with other nations because he believed it would compromise the religious as well as the political freedom of his country. He was a genius, a poet-seer, and a man of action. His ministry lasted for more than a generation because of his energy involvement.

Israel was taken into exile by the Babylonians, but God remembered His Covenant promises, and Isaiah exclaimed this message to the people of Israel. God would exonerate and deliver Israel from sin. *"For Zion's sake I will not keep silent, and for Jerusalem's sake I will not rest, until her vindication shines out like the dawn, and her salvation like a burning torch"* (Isaiah 62: 1). Isaiah reassures the people that God would return them to their Promised Land. *"You shall no more be termed Forsaken" for I, the Lord will be with you. You shall be called "My Delight Is in Her" for you will obey My statutes and commandments. "And your land shall be called Beulah" for it will be as if your land was married to Me, and I will bless it, and make it prosperous and plentiful. "And as the bridegroom rejoices over the bride, so shall your God rejoice over you"* (Isaiah 62: 5).

We Live in a World that is Controlled by the Energy of God and Our Commitment to Serve God Deals with Our Energy Involvement in What We are Trying to Do

"Holy, holy, holy is the Lord of hosts; the whole earth is full of His glory" (Isaiah 6:3). The theology of the Black Nation Israel and of the Prophet Isaiah—theology being a body of beliefs concerning God and man's relation-

ship with God—was that God was transcendent, everywhere and in everything, "the sole Creator of the universe, Lord of history, Savior of Israel His chosen people and, indeed all of mankind" (*Bible Dictionary*). This concept that the whole earth is full of His glory denotes an energy field, not a super being. This is further explained by our Holy Patriarch, Jaramogi Abebe Agyeman who teaches that, "God is the Cosmic Energy and Creative Intelligence out of which all things were created. All energy is unified in a single energy field, which is God. Everything in the universe is energy" *(BCN Message and Mission)*, So, the world is controlled by the energy of God. This control can be viewed in the rising of the sun.

Have you ever seen the sun rise over a sleeping lake?
The lake is dimly dark and the sounds of life quiet.
Slowly the sun emerges.
And penetrates the darkness,
Bringing light with its ascent.
Its rays reflect upon the sleeping lake, and colors it,
from dimly dark, to a blend of vivid blue and green.
The fish swim and the waves sway.
The birds sing and man awakes.
God, again, brings a new day!

Our commitment to serve God deals with our energy involvement in what we are trying to do. Being created out of the substance of God, we are energy beings born with the capacity to contact the power of God which is available to us. When we apply heat to a pot of water, the water first begins to move, then to slightly bubble, then vigorously bubble and boil. One form of energy (heat) was applied to another form (water) and the effects resulted in a higher energy state for the water. In the same sense, when we have faith (one form of energy) and apply it with actions (another form of energy), we have an heightened energy involvement in building the Black Nation, God's Kingdom on earth, to meet the crises of our survival. Without an energy involvement, spiritually and physically we wither away as a Nation for we have lost contact with the energy (power) of God. We become only a "shell of a person", apathetic, negative and choosing a path of least resistance. We run from group confrontation, we give up, become lazy, and slow moving. We slowly die! The nation dies!

The energy level rises when people
commit themselves to doing something;
to solving the problems"

–Jaramogi

We Believe in Beulah Land as the Promised Land, and We will Sacrifice and Fight for It because it is the Will of God

"If you do not stand firm in faith, you shall not stand at all" (Isaiah 7: 9). In light of the conditions threatening our survival, we must renew our faith and believe in Beulah Land as the Promised Land. We have no other choice, but to believe in the Covenant promise of God that we will possess our own land. The land will be married to God for God will dwell in it with us as we commit ourselves to being His Holy People. "The Lord has proclaimed to the end of the earth: We shall be called, *'The Holy People, The Redeemed of the Lord'* (Isaiah 61:11, 12).

Beulah Land is our answer to the problems confronting Black people. It offers an opportunity for communal living. In communal living, there is an equitable distribution of tasks, affection, and spiritual energy; here energy involvement will be high. In such an environment, the needs of Black people will be met. The physical needs of food, shelter, and clothing will be supplied. The emotional needs of "belonging," "being accepted", and "being loved" will be fulfilled. The aspirations of finding a meaning and purpose in life will be fulfilled. Beulah Land will provide a home, a place where Black people feel cared for. Beulah Land offers an opportunity for a better future for all young adults and children.

Even though our children have been mis-educated, and very few opportunities are left for young Black graduates, all is not lost because Beulah Land will provide a home for all of our children. Being free of the dangers and lures of the city and unemployment, Beulah Land will be furnished with a school, and activities and work that will nurture the growth and security of our young. They will be able to grow and be all that God intended them to be. They, too will commit their lives to God's Promised Land, and pass it on to their children.

Beulah Land offers a sensible involvement in the machinery of the world in which we live. However, Black people tend not to try. If it seems like no one else is trying, we do not try. Many of us are not dealing with the problem. We engage ourselves in small jobs, and schools to find some opportunities but these attempts are futile. Beulah Land can change this mode of thinking and acting. For any Black person who has a little hope left, there is something we can do about the world in which we live. We can provide a place for Black people, as conditions get worse. Those having a difficult time trying to make it will find security on Beulah Land. The gates of Beulah Land will be open to absorb all Black people. Its purpose is not to be elitist, catering only to the intellectually superior. We fight with the belief that God did not create us to be slaves, to be homeless, to be hungry or to be denied opportunities to live an abundant life. We must fight now, and sacrifice for Beulah Land. As this was the will of God with Israel, so it is the will of God with us!

Beulah Land is strategically necessary. This is it! We must make it work or the Nation will not survive the conditions facing Black people, also directly affecting each one of us, including our children. We are not immune to the conditions in America, but we can build while we have time!

We Believe the Fullest Expression of Our Covenant is Our Commitment to Build Beulah Land. We Bring to This Commitment and Struggle All of Our Energy of Our Faith in God

We are all now being tested on our belief in the Covenant. Will we rise to the occasion of building Beulah Land believing God will be with us? Our commitment to do this is shown by our energy involvement in doing all that is necessary to build our Promised Land! Since 1981, we have been raising and saving money for Beulah Land. None of this money has been spent, but soon will be. We must supply seed, fertilizer, farm machinery, housing and food for the first Beulah Land cadre. As produce is harvested, the three regions will be supplied and the surplus will be sold or furnished to those in need. As Beulah Land develops, more housing for adults and children, more schools, more machinery, and canning facilities will be needed.

We commit ourselves today! We bring to this commitment and struggle all of our faith in God. Our faith undergirds our actions. We do what we believe! For the building of Beulah Land, we need money; we need people to seriously work on Beulah Land; we need to discuss and solve the problems; we need to mobilize our groups and the region to meet the crises in these next ten years. Everything we do must be geared for the building of Beulah Land. To be in the Nation today, means you support Beulah Land. As we bring to this all of our energy, the energy level of the Nation will rise, and affect Black people across the world. A faithful few can make miracles! Let us strengthen our faith in God! *"You who remind the Lord, take no rest, and give Him no rest until He establishes Beulah Land and makes it renowned throughout the earth."* (Isaiah 62:6).

THE BIRTH OF A SUPERIOR PEOPLE

"Be conscious of the divinity within you...Thank GOD, who made us the most beautiful people, The most powerful people and the best of people."

—Jaramogi

NKURUMAH KESEE: Greatness, superiority or supremacy. *A well-mannered person or character.*

> *"But you are a chosen race a royal priesthood a holy nation God's own people, in order that you may proclaim the mighty acts of Him who called you out of darkness into His marvelous light."*
>
> (1st Peter 2:9)

Bible Lesson: During the time of Peter's letter (64 A.D.), the severity of Roman oppression and persecution of Christians forced many to escape from Jerusalem. He sends them a letter of hope reminding them of their relationship with God, and their loyalty to the mission of Jesus, the Black Messiah. He begins, *"To the exiles of the Dispersion in Pontus, Galatia, Cappadocia, Asia, and Bitkynia, who have been chosen and destined by God the Father and sanctified by the Spirit to be obedient to Jesus Christ...may grace and peace be yours in abundance"* (1st Peter 1:1). He calls them to righteous living. *"Therefore prepare your minds for action; discipline yourselves; set all your hope on the grace that Jesus Christ will bring you when he is revealed. Like obedient children, do not be conformed to the desires that you formerly had in ignorance. Instead, as he who called you is holy, be holy yourselves in all your conduct; for it is written, 'You shall be holy, for I am holy"* (1st Peter 1:13-14). He reminds them of what they must do to be holy. *'Rid yourselves, therefore, of all malice, and all* *guile, insincerity, envy, and all slander'* (1st Peter 2:1). Peter then reassures them that they are a superior people set apart because of their allegiance to God, their righteous values and behaviors, and their love for each other. *"But you are a chosen race, a royal priesthood, a holy nation."*

25 Years Ago, a Different Reality Existed for Black People

Denied by law to ride in the front of the bus, to eat at certain restaurants, to attend certain schools, to live in certain neighborhoods, and to vote, was the reality of Black people who were alienated from White America. We had no rights that White people recognized. This motivated a small percentage of Black people to organize and propel a Civil Rights Movement (1955-1965) to gain protection by the Constitution for all Black people, and to remove all barriers which restricted us from full participation in society. It was a struggle to end our oppression. Nonviolent protests, boycotts, and rallies were staged to bring attention to this issue.

This was the reality for those who joined the Pan African Orthodox Christian Church during or shortly after 1965. We believed that Black people had an enemy, and we had to build a Nation of our own. We sought to end identification with White people, so we chose to wear Afro hairstyles as a rejection of western standards of beauty. More Black people wore African dress, jewelry, and dashikis. The slogan "Black Power" reflected our intent to build our own, and to have input in regards to our own history. Our founders and early members were actively engaged in sit-ins to protest the mis-education of Black children. They published the Illustrated News to inform Black people of our conditions and problems. They politically endorsed candidates for office to legislate on behalf of Black people. These were actions of a people who did not feel a part of America. It was a different reality!

Today, Black People Feel More of A Part of America

The atrocities and hostile resistance of Whites against Black people in the Civil Rights Struggle were televised nationally and internationally. The whole world watched as Black men, women, and children were injured by powerful blasts of water from fire hoses, beaten brutally by White police, bitten by attack dogs, dragged into police wagons, jailed and murdered. This attention brought some pressure upon the federal government to intervene. Over a period of years, changes in legislation occurred, some of which were desegregation, affirmative action, and the right to vote. We were allowed to attend all schools and universities, to work in corporate

America, to ride in the front of the bus, to live in all neighborhoods, to spend money and to go anywhere. We believed that everything we fought for, we gained. Our reality had changed! Before, we did not feel a part of America. Now, we do! We feel now that we are real citizens. For the majority of Black people, freedom has been won; the struggle is over.

Today, we feel we do not have to do anything! We have the right to do what we want to, to state our own opinions, to do our own thing, to even be criminals. Feeling we have nothing to struggle for, we have grown more individualistic and materialistic; we are alienated from one another. Our lives are filled with broken relationships, tension, anxiety, and insecurity. We find ways to escape (drugs, school, and otherworldly religion) while pretending to be happy. We are grasping in the wind for fulfillment, but like the wind, it passes right through our hands.

> *"You have already spent enough time in doing what the Gentiles like to do, living in Licentiousness, passions, drunkenness, revels, carousing, and lawless idolatry."*
>
> (1st Peter 4-3)

The Role of the Pan African Orthodox Christian Church is to Build a Superior People

"For those who desire life and desire to see good days, let them keep their tongues from evil and their lips from speaking deceit; let them turn away from evil and do good; let them seek peace and pursue it. For the eyes of the Lord are on the righteous, and His ears are open to their prayer. But the face of the Lord is against those who do evil" (1st Peter 3:10-12). The PAOCC accepts the responsibility to build a superior people who have overcome the temptations of the slave culture (individualism, materialism, and escapism), and who accept communalism as a fulfillment of a people's life. KUA: **The Science of Becoming What You Already Are** begins with you becoming a part of a group. Socialization is the process to move people from individualism to communalism. Because we are born as individual beings, there is a tendency to grow more and more individualistic (going out of control) which alienates us from each other; this alienation is sinful and prevents us from establishing a relationship with God. Socialization can only occur when a person involves himself in the life of the group. This involvement helps him/her to resist the ways of the slave culture, which are destructive, and transforms him to accept a new life in which he learns to love, where he

feels he belongs and in which he accepts the responsibility of building a decent world for Black people by building a Black Nation. *"Finally, all of you have unity of spirit, sympathy, love for one another, a tender heart, and a humble mind. Do not repay evil for evil or abuse for abuse; but, on the contrary, repay with a blessing"* (1st Peter 3: 8). Superiority is acquired through the **rebirth** of a people who have rejected individualism (Satan) and all its evil ways, and who have been touched by God.... A *chosen race, a royal priesthood, a holy nation, God's own people.*

WE SHARE A SACRED TRUST

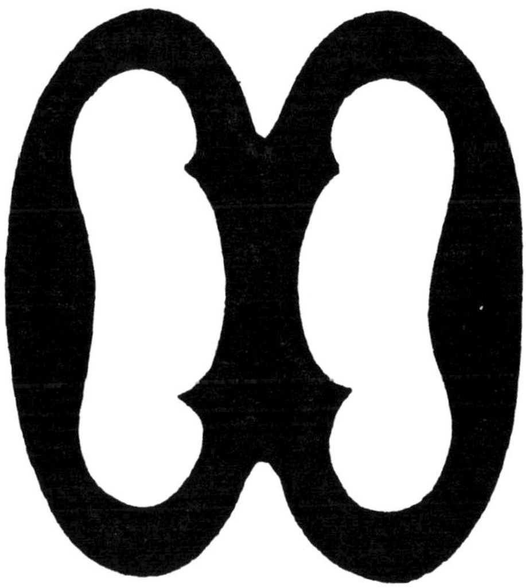

"We share a sacred trust with those who have gone before and those who will come after. We are in total submission to the will of GOD." Kujitoa

—Kutafuta Ritual

NKONSONKONSON: Unity, responsibility, interdependence, brotherhood, and cooperation.
A chain or link

"And Joshua said to all the people, 'Thus says the Lord, the God of Israel. Long ago your ancestors—Terah and his sons Abraham and Nahor—lived beyond the Euphrates and served other gods. Then I took your father Abraham from beyond the River and led him through all the land of Canaan and made his offspring many ... I gave you a land on which you had not labored, and towns that you had not built, and you live in them; you eat the fruit of vineyards and olive yards that you did not plant. Now therefore revere the Lord, and serve him in sincerity and in faithfulness; put away the gods that your ancestors served beyond the River and in Egypt, and serve the Lord. Now if you are unwilling to serve the Lord, choose this day whom you will serve, whether the gods your ancestors served in the region beyond the River or the gods of the Amorites in whose land you are living; but as for me and my household, we will serve the Lord."

(Joshua 24: 2-5; 14-15)

Bible Lesson: After the death of Moses, servant of the Lord, Joshua succeeded him as the leader of Israel. "The Lord spoke to Joshua, now proceed to cross the Jordan, you and all this people, into the land that I am giving to the Israelites. No one shall be able to stand against you all the days of your life. As I was with Moses, so I will be with you. Only be strong and very courageous, being careful to act in accordance with all the law that My servant Moses commanded you" (Joshua 1:1-7). Joshua is called by God to maintain a sacred trust with Moses, who had gone on before, through obedience to the Covenant. The Covenant is what bound Joshua to God and to his people as he continued the sacred task of nation building. He led the armies of Israel into battle to conquer the Promised Land. Under his leadership, thirty-one kings and their nations were defeated. Joshua then assigned portions of land to the twelve tribes of Israel. In his life, he had done what God expected, possessing the Promised Land, fighting battles, mobilizing his people, making political-religious decisions, and holding Israel to the Covenant as one people.

Joshua advanced in years, and grew old. Being aware of his days left upon the earth, he summoned all the tribes of Israel, the elders, the heads, the judges and officers to the Ceremony of the Renewal of the Covenant. He recalls their history reminding them of all that God had done. From the call of Abraham, to their deliverance from Egyptian oppression, to the parting of the Red Sea, to God's protection in the wilderness, and their conquest of the Promised Land, Joshua reminds them that God kept His promises of the Covenant. They had conquered nations who had built great cities, had planted lush gardens, and developed great agriculture. God says, *"I gave you a land on which you had not labored, and towns that you had not built, and you live in them; you eat the fruit of vineyards and olive yards that you did not plant"* (Joshua 24:13). Joshua tells Israel what is required of them in maintaining their Covenant relationship with God. *"Now therefore revere the Lord, and serve Him in sincerity and in faithfulness..."* Joshua demanded that they make a decision. "Choose this day whom you will serve." Serving God was more than a mere statement; it was the only force, which would hold them together as a nation. Without the shared Covenant and obedience to God as a people, Israel could do nothing, but degenerate into individualism contributing to their own demise. Joshua implores them to make a decision for the survival of their nation depended on this. He repudiates all other gods and tells the whole assembly what his decision is. *"As for me and my household, we will serve the Lord."'*

> *"Take good care to observe the commandment and instructions that Moses the servant of the Lord commanded you, to love the Lord your God, to walk in all His ways."*
>
> (Joshua 22:5)

In Every Generation, God Calls Those Who Hear to Give Commitment to the Covenant

Since the beginning of time, God has demanded that mankind, His own creation, live righteously and in obedience to His will. *"The Lord loves those who hate evil; He guards the lives of His faithful; He rescues them from the hand of the wicked. Light dawns for the righteous, and joy for the upright in heart"* (Psalm 10-11). *"If you will only obey the Lord your God, by diligently observing all His commandments that I am commanding you today, the Lord your God will set you high above all the nations of the earth...if you obey the Lord your God"* (Deuteronomy 28:1-2). Upon this religious premise of righteousness and obedience, God called the Black Nation Israel into being to be His holy people, and to build His kingdom on earth; a kingdom where love, harmony, communalism, freedom and righteousness prevailed. How can this be done? Only through the acceptance of a Covenant relationship with God, which commits a people to religious obligations in order to maintain a relationship with God, and at the same time commits God to protect, bless, and deliver them. The Covenant is the system of beliefs, the force, which keeps a people united in mind and action; it is the means of their survival and their salvation; it is their reason to become a nation dedicated to the will of God.

In every generation, God calls those who hear to give commitment to the Covenant. In 1953, God called our founders. They faced a world in which Black people were discriminated and excluded. By law, the Supreme Court ruled "separate but equal," so every aspect of the Black man's life was segregated from White America. However, it was not equal. We were denied the right to vote, the opportunity to a better education, the choice to live in decent housing, the opportunity to better jobs and pay, and to quality medical care. We were relegated to a life of poverty and ignorance. Life, liberty, and the pursuit of happiness were denied by the oppressive system we lived in. Black people were in trouble and needed help! God observed the misery of our people, and indeed knew our sufferings, and saw how America oppressed us. God called our founders; they heard and they responded. God showed them that the traditional church, (taking people to a pie in the sky when they die) was not relevant to the Black man's condition on earth; therefore, they began to create a new church with the belief that God was concerned about a "people." So, the church's mission was to do the same. They accepted the Covenant; *"I'll be your God if you will be My people."* Like Joshua, they repudiated all other gods and other churches that did not follow the Covenant.

Walking out of the Saint Mark's Presbyterian Church, they were determined to build a new church that was relevant to the every day, hour-by-hour, needs of Black people. They welcomed Black people into the church and by their love and sincerity gave Black people a "sense of belonging"; they taught and discussed issues with the youth broadening their understanding of their condition and what they must do for Black people; they held sit-ins protesting discrimination; they developed Black teacher organizations to deal with the problem of miseducation; they organized politically to get people into office who were concerned about the welfare of Black people; they organized the Inner City Organizing Committee to fight against injustice. Jaramogi, founder and Holy Patriarch of the Shrines of the Black Madonna, speaks today on the founders of yesterday. *"We hereby establish this church to express our commitment to God. We do this through the church."* Our founders committed their lives to the Covenant, and did what they had to do in their time.

"But as for me and my household,
we will serve the Lord."

In This Generation, Our Task is to Create a Means of Survival in which We are Not Dependent Upon the Safety Net Provided by the Government or White Liberal Benevolence

In every generation, God calls those who hear to confront and deal with the existing conditions. Our founders dealt with the problem of discrimination and exclusion. In our generation, feelings are different than the time of our founders. It is felt today that "separate but equal" (segregation) is no longer the problem. The feeling is that we are "included." The issues of voting, equal schooling, fair living accommodations, America and many Black people feel have been resolved. So it is felt that Black people no longer need the assistance of government in welfare, in fair practices, in equal opportunities (safety net). As a result, affirmative action has been declared unconstitutional, and there has been a drastic decline of Black youth in higher education professional schools; welfare has and is being reformed in all the states, and thousands are without food, shelter, and health care; federal and state funding are not being channeled to urban schools, and our children still receive an inferior education. *"Although the Black man still needs help and doesn't have an equal position, the government and the majority of White people feel Black people have come far enough"* (Jaramogi). This puts a whole new face on the struggle!

Today, we are trying to survive without government assistance even though we still need it in our struggle for equality. This is the basic difference in the conditions faced by our founders and in those faced by us. *"Now, we are charged by God to create a means of survival without the historical dependency upon the safety nets provided by the government and liberal White people"* (Jaramogi). God is calling us to change our values, to transform our relationships, and to commit our resources of time, money, and skills to meet the needs of our people. God is calling those who hear to accept the task of providing our own safety nets for our people with a sense of urgency.

Some have heard the call of God and did not act accordingly for personal reasons: I must get myself together first; I don't have time; I have my own goals. Others have ears to hear, but their hearing is impaired by individualism so what they hear is what they want God to say; God said He would bless me with a car. With some, God's call fell on theologically confused minds, so they question if it was God or not; "God certainly wouldn't call me to build a nation for my people." "He isn't in nation business; He's in the saving business!" God is calling us today, and for those who hear, we must **commit** our lives to the Covenant now and forever.

We share a sacred trust with those who have gone before and with those who will come after."
—Jaramogi

The Black Man is in a Dilemma by Which He Can Extricate Himself Only by Recognizing That The Power of God is Available Through the Realistic Use of Communalism as a Total Religious Way of Life

The Black man can only disentangle himself from the conditions threatening our survival by recognizing that the Power of God is available. This recognition would not only serve as a means of survival, but also as reconciliation for failing to keep our sacred trust with those who have gone before and with those who will come after. The spiritual power needed to change our conditions is available if we structure love and communalism into every aspect of our daily lives. Why would one struggle for the life of another? Why would we even want to carry on the struggle started by our founders? Why would we strive to keep the Covenant? LOVE! Jesus said, *"No one has greater love than this, to lay down one's life for one's friends"* (John 15:13). We must see each other as friends and be willing to sacrifice our individualism for the survival of our people. Expressions of love in concrete acts make us aware of the spiritual reality we live in and create a new dimension to how we think and feel. Love opens us to God. Acts of kindness, compassion, and concern are built into the group process. So, the group helps us to Love again! The disciplines of KUA, the worship service, the devotionals, tear down the walls that separate us and we become aware of the spiritual union we share with one another and with God.

Why communalism? It is the only means for equality in which members give as they have, and receive, as they need. Everyone can enjoy the abundance of life with food, shelter, clothing, health and happiness. A communal society offers security from the cradle to the grave because it recognizes the God-given value of each person. Only through the equal distribution of affection and tasks can we realistically build institutions to take care of the needs of our people. The Missionary Training Institutes, the Kuumba Kitchen, the Alkebu-lan Nursery and Mtoto House, the Cultural Centers are institutions built by communalism! Sacrifice of time, money and skills brought these institutions into reality. Love and communalism is our only way of keeping the Covenant and of sharing a sacred trust with our founders! Our work is not over! We are charged by God to build a Nation! We can! We will!

Will you say today, *"As for me and my house, we will serve the Lord!"*

COMMUNALISM: THE CHOICE OF THE RIGHTEOUS

"The nature of GOD is unity as reflected in the interpendency of GOD's creation."

—Jaramogi

AKOMA NTOASO: Agreement, togetherness and unity in thought and in deed. Joined or united hearts.

> *"These are the descendants of Noah. Noah was a righteous man blameless in his generation; Noah walked with God. And Noah had three sons, Shem, Ham, and Japheth. Now the earth was corrupt in God's sight, and the earth was filled with violence. And God saw that the earth was corrupt...And God said to them; now I am going to destroy them along with the earth. Make yourself an ark."*
>
> (Genesis 6:14)

Bible Lesson: *"Noah was a righteous man, blameless in his generation; Noah walked with God."* We must ask ourselves, "What is righteous in the sight of God?" The answer can be drawn from the revelations given to the prophets, to Jesus, and to the apostles of the First Christian Church. *"For I the Lord love justice. I hate robbery and wrongdoing"* (Isaiah 61:8). *"But as for you, return to your God. Hold fast to love and justice, and wait continually for your God"* (Hosea 12:6). Jesus said, *"The Spirit of the Lord, is upon me, because He has anointed me to bring good news to the poor, to proclaim release to the captives, and recovery of sight to the blind, to let the oppressed go free"* (Luke 4:18). Jesus also said, *"Love one another...by this everyone will know you are my disciples"* (John 13:35), The work of the First Christian Church was to continue the mission of Jesus through teaching, preaching, healing, and communal living. *"Awe came upon everyone, because many wonders and signs were being done by the apostles. All who believed were together and had all things in common; they would sell their possessions and goods and distribute the proceeds to all, as any had need"* (Acts 2:43-44). In essence, justice, love, seeking God and communal living are righteous in the sight of God.

What is evil is characterized by unrestrained behaviors of individualism. *"These people, however, are like, irrational animals, mere creatures of instinct. They slander what they do not understand. They have eyes full of adultery, insatiable for sin. They speak bombastic nonsense, and with licentious (sexually unrestrained, immoral) desires of the flesh, they entice people who have just escaped from those who live in error"* (2nd Peter 2). From these spring, oppression, injustice, hate, corruption, and self-indulgence. This was the wickedness of man during the time of Noah. *"The Lord saw that the wickedness of humankind was great in the earth, and that every inclination of the thoughts of their hearts was only evil continually, and the Lord was sorry that He had made humankind on earth."* (Genesis 6:3-6) The Lord does make a distinction between the righteous and the wicked. God tells Noah to build an ark for, *"I will blot out from the earth the human beings I have created."* Noah obeys God and takes his wife, his three sons and their wives, and the male and female of every living creature. God spares Noah and his family because of Noah's righteousness, and God tells him, "I will establish my covenant with you."

God blesses the righteous,
but the wicked shall perish.

Introduction: "God *is Cosmic Energy* and *Creative Intelligence, the Unified Energy Field out of* which all *things were* and *are created.* The nature of God *is* **UNITY,** as reflected in the *Interdependency of all of God's creation.* In light of this, human life consists of a basic struggle between **individualism** and communalism. ***History*** *records this struggle."*

Jaramogi
BCN Body of Knowledge

Individualism is a Satanic Force in the World Today, and has Virtually Replaced a God Centered View in Which Everything was Sacred

"And God saw that the earth was corrupt; for all flesh had corrupted its ways upon the earth."

Jaramogi teaches that, "God is Cosmic Energy and Creative Intelligence, the Unified

Energy Field out of which all things are created." This perception of God is supported by the Bible. *In the beginning God created the heavens and the earth. The earth was a formless void"* (Genesis 1:1). *"God breathed into man's nostrils the breath of life, and man became a living being"* (Genesis 2:7). This perception of God discounts God as being a man (anthropomorphic), but that God is the "Great Spirit"—"The Energy Field"—which permeates all of the cosmos. African people were the first to come upon this reality that God is everywhere and in everything; therefore, everything on the earth, the animals, the sky, the fish, the rivers, the flowers and vegetables were all sacred. This belief motivated our people to seek a relationship with God (Power and Energy), and a communal relationship with others. The rituals of African people were designed to OPEN individuals to the flowing energy of God. The communal lifestyle in which all were treated with importance, and resources were shared for the good of all, was an out pouring of love, justice, welfare, and compassion; a positive energy flow to others which was both healing and ensured our survival. Communalism is a reflection of the LOVE of God.

In the 15th Century, this God-centered view of the world began to crumble as Europeans emerged from their Dark Ages and relentlessly, and aggressively annihilated, enslaved and oppressed African people as well as other people of color. With European expansion came a "New Primitive Age of Individualism" that swept across the world like a tidal wave. They declared that we were inferior, and so declared our rituals. They slandered communalism declaring it to be primitive. Black people have not recovered from this onslaught of Satanic forces, and the world is in shambles on a collision course headed for disaster. Nothing is sacred in the world! The air, soil, and water have been polluted because of the individualistic greed of those in power who allow pesticides and insecticides to drain into the lakes and rivers killing the life of the waters. Giant landfills have been dug into the earth where tons of garbage and toxic waste are dumped, and the poison seep into the soil, absorbed by plants, and eaten by humans. The earth has been transformed into a huge garbage can. Once created to give life, it now sows death. Nothing is sacred in the world! The desires of the flesh, the lower nature of man, are uncontrolled because of individualism. So, from the youngest to the oldest, the poorest to the richest, from the "hood" to the Capital, CORRUPTION thrives! Child molestation in the Catholic Church, licentiousness on TV, adultery in Buckingham Place, lies in the Church, psychotic massacres at work-sites, and children fighting parents are all symptoms of a world in bondage to the Satanic force of Individualism, Sadly, our Motherland has succumbed to this grave sin. One African leader had assets of five billion to eight billion dollars, while only 10% of the roads in Zaire are paved, and over 50% of the children die before the age of five. *"And the Lord, was sorry that He had made humankind on the earth, and it grieved Him to His heart."* (Genesis 6:8)

If We are to Fulfill the Covenant and Live in Obedience to God, We Must First Find Our Way Back to Man's Original State of Being at the Time of Creation

"We are energy beings created out of the same substance as God!" (Jaramogi). At the time of creation, we were OPEN to God, which gave us a higher consciousness. In this state, we were in harmony with God manifesting peace, love, health, and happiness. We were enlightened to the spiritual reality all around us, and to the incarnate God within each human being. Jaramogi states, *"The quest, to return to this original state of being pits man in a struggle, to overcome their individualism as they, seek to obey God by building a Communal Society or the Kingdom of God on earth.* " The Kung Tribe of Africa is an example of this.

"For the Kung, healing is more than the application of medicine. Healing seeks to establish health and growth on physical, psy-

chological, social, and spiritual levels; it involves work on the individual, the group, and the surrounding environment and cosmos. Healing pervades Kung culture, as a fundamental integrating and enhancing force. The culture's emphasis on sharing and egalitarianism; its vital life of the Spirit and strong Community, are expressed in and supported by the healing tradition. The central event in this tradition is the all-night healing dance.

"Four times a month on the average, night signals the start of a healing dance. The women sit around the fire, singing and rhythmically, clapping. The men, sometimes joined by women, dance around the singers. As the dance intensifies, num or Spiritual Energy is activated in the healers, both men and women, but mostly among the dancing men. As num is activated in them, they begin to *kia* or experience an enhancement of their consciousness. While experiencing kia, they heal all those at the dance. Before the sun rises fully the next morning, the dance usually ends. Those at the dance find it exciting, joyful, and powerful. 'Being at a dance makes our hearts happy, the Kung say'" (*Boiling Energy*).

If Christians today are to live by the Covenant, "I 'll be your God if you will be my people," then we must return to an OPEN state of being just as the Kung where we can experience God and community.

KUA is the Process Which Returns Us to Our Original State of Being and Opens Us Both to Community and to God

"KUA leads you to become what you already are, capable of being open to the Cosmic Power of God, the Spiritual Energy Field in which we live" (Jaramogi). What must we do? We must take being a Christian more seriously. Like Jesus, we must seek the experience of God. It is our thirst for God that influences us to attend worship service, devotionals, and KUA workshops designed to OPEN us to God. Like Jesus, we must renounce individualism. Only our hunger for justice, love, and peace, all the things that God loves, can drive us to reject the Satanic force of individualism. Facing the reality that we too are a part of the Satanic force when we use the Nation, seeking all the benefits, but not contributing time, money and skills, yet expect all kinds of considerations for our circumstances; when we sacrifice for our individual desires, but not for the group's goals and obligations; when we are unwilling to resolve conflicts; when we treat others in a mean and condescending way, should inspire us to seek change in an urgent way. We then can accept the group as the only entity, which can move us from individualism to communalism. Like the disciples at Pentecost, who committed their lives to building the

Kingdom of God on earth by "giving as they had and receiving as they had need," we are charged to do the same. Only our honesty and sincerity will launch us on the mission to change the world by first being changed ourselves. Then, we will support all the institutions of the Church and declare them to be our own.

KUA in the Pan African Orthodox Christian Church can lead a seeker to righteousness and communal living. Will you seek today? Will you take God seriously? Will you take communalism seriously? If so, then like Noah, the Lord will say, "You are righteous, and you walk with Me." Build yourself an Ark out of Black Christian Nationalism, and I will bless you and spare your lives. I will make a Covenant between you and Me, and you will become a great nation bringing the world, its government, and all its institutions into conformity with My will. It is God who speaks!

BIBLIOGRAPHY

Bethel, Elizabeth. *Promiseland: A Century of Life in a Negro Community.* South Carolina: South Carolina Press, 1997.

Borg, Marcus. *Jesus A New Vision.* San Francisco: HarperCollins, 1987.

Bramly, Serge. *Macumba.* New York: St. Martin's Press, 1977.

Carson, C., Garrow, D., Gill, V., Harding, V., Hine, D. *The Eyes on the Prize Civil Rights Reader*, Massachusetts: Blackslide, Inc., 1987.

Chicago Sun Times, 1997.

Chopra, Deepak. *Perfect Health.* New York: Harmony Books, 1991.

Chopra, Deepak. *Creating Health.* Massachusetts: Houghton Mifflin Co., 1987.

Cleage, Albert B. Jr. *The Black Messiah.* New Jersey: Africa World Press, Inc., 2nd Printing 1981.

Cleage, Albert B. *Black Christian Nationalism.* New York: William Morrow & Company, 1972.

Cleage, Albert B. *BCN Message and Mission,* 1987.

Cleage, Albert B. *BCN Teaches,* 1972.

Cleage, Albert B. *Tribute Booklet,* 1995.
Cleage, Albert B. *BCN Manisfesto,* 1953.
Cleage, Albert B. *BCN Body of Knowledge,* 1991.
Cleage, Albert B. *BCN Statement of Faith,* 1972.
Cleage, Albert B. *BCN Creed.*
Eisenman, R., Wise, M. *The Dead Sea Scrolls.* Massachusetts: Element,1992.
Franklin, John and Moss, Alfred, Jr. *From Slavery to Freedom.* New York: McGraw-Hill, Inc., 6th edition, 1988.
Hills, Christopher. *Creative Conflict.* California: University of the Trees Press, 1980.
Houston Chronicle Magazine (1998). The Theory of Everything.
Houston Chronicle (1997).
Interpreter's Dictionary to the Bible, 19th ed. Tennessee: Abingdon Press, 1991.
Katz, Richard. *Boiling Energy.* Massachusetts: Harvard University Press, 1982.
Knoke, William. *Bold New World.* New York: Kodansha International,1996.
Kozol, Jonathan. *Savage Inequalities.* New York: Harper Perennial, 1991.
Kozol, Jonathan. *Amazing Grace.* New York: Harper Perennial, 1995.
Manning, Marable. *How Capitalism Underdeveloped Black America.* Massachusetts, 1983.

Marks, Carole. *Farewell: We're Good and Gone, The Great Black Migration.* Indianapolis: Indiana University Press, 1989.

Mbiti, John S. *African Religions and Philosophy:* New York: Doubleday Company, Inc., 1969.

New Jerusalem Bible. New York: Doubleday and Company, Inc., 1967.

Schonfield, Hugh. *The Essene Odyssey.* Great Britain: Element, 1984.

Schonfield, Hugh. *The Jesus Party.* New York: Macmillan Publishing Co., 1974.

Silk, 1992.

Szekely, Edmond Bordeaux. *TheEssene Origins of Christianity.* The International Biogenic Society, 1993.

Trefil, 1983.

Unger, Merrill. *The New Unger's Bible Dictionary.* Chicago: Moody Press, 4th edition, 1988.